First World War
and Army of Occupation
War Diary
France, Belgium and Germany

26 DIVISION
77 Infantry Brigade
Headquarters,
Royal Scots Fusiliers 8th Battalion,
Black Watch (Royal Highlanders) 10th Battalion,
Cameronians (Scottish Rifles) 11th Battalion
and Princess Louise's (Argyll & Sutherland Highlanders)
12th Battalion
1 September 1914 - 31 October 1915

WO95/2253/1

The Naval & Military Press Ltd
www.nmarchive.com
Published in association with The National Archives

Published by

The Naval & Military Press Ltd

Unit 10 Ridgewood Industrial Park,

Uckfield, East Sussex,

TN22 5QE England

Tel: +44 (0) 1825 749494

www.naval-military-press.com

www.nmarchive.com

This diary has been reprinted in facsimile from the original. Any imperfections are inevitably reproduced and the quality may fall short of modern type and cartographic standards.

© **Crown Copyright**
Images reproduced by permission of The National Archives, London, England, 2015.

Contents

Document type	Place/Title	Date From	Date To
Heading	WO95/2253/1		
Heading	26th Division 77th Infy Bde Bde Headquarters 8th Bn Roy Scots Fus. 11th Bn Scottish Rif. 10th Bn Black Watch 12th Bn Arg. & Suth. Hdrs Sep-Oct 1915		
Heading	On His Majesty's Service. 26th Division Headquarters 77th Inf Bde Vol 2 Sept-Oct 15		
Heading	26th Division Headquarters 77th Inf. Brigade Vol I Sept 15		
Miscellaneous	The Adjutant General Base	04/10/1915	04/10/1915
War Diary	Sherrington	01/09/1914	01/09/1914
War Diary	Sulton Veny	01/09/1915	18/09/1915
War Diary	Folkestone	19/09/1915	19/09/1915
War Diary	Boulogne	20/09/1915	20/09/1915
War Diary	Fricamps	21/09/1915	22/09/1915
War Diary	Pont De Metz	23/09/1915	23/09/1915
War Diary	Villers Bretonneux	24/09/1915	30/09/1915
Heading	War Diary Of 77th Infantry Brigade From 1st October 1915 To 31st October 1915 Volume II		
War Diary	Villers Bretonneux	01/10/1915	11/10/1915
War Diary	Sailly Lorette	12/10/1915	14/10/1915
War Diary	Bray	15/10/1915	28/10/1915
War Diary	Sailly Lorette	29/10/1915	29/10/1915
War Diary	Villers Bocage	30/10/1915	31/10/1915
Miscellaneous	7th Brigade App 1	01/10/1915	01/10/1915
Miscellaneous	Attachment Of 77th And 79th Brigade App 1		
War Diary	77th Infantry Brigade App 1	02/10/1915	02/10/1915
Miscellaneous	A Form Messages And Signals Appendix 2		
Miscellaneous	77th Infantry Brigade Appendix 3	09/10/1915	09/10/1915
Operation(al) Order(s)	5th Division Operation Order No. 72 App 4	10/10/1915	10/10/1915
Miscellaneous	Table Of Moves-(Issued With 5th Division Operation Order No. 72 App 4		
Miscellaneous	5th Division G.B. 56/1 App 4	11/10/1915	11/10/1915
Operation(al) Order(s)	Extract From 5th Division Operation Order No. 72 App 5		
Miscellaneous	Table Of Moves (Issued With 5th Division Operation Order No 72 App 5		
Miscellaneous	12		
Miscellaneous	Move Orders 77th Brigade App 6	11/10/1915	11/10/1915
Miscellaneous	App 7	12/10/1915	12/10/1915
Miscellaneous	5th Division G.B. 56 App 7	11/10/1915	11/10/1915
Miscellaneous	13th		
Miscellaneous	Table Of Moves (Issued With 15th Inf. Bde. Operation Order No. 10) App 7A		
Miscellaneous	15th Bde Orders		
Miscellaneous	Moves On 15th Instant Will Be As Follows:- 5th Division G.B. 56/2 App 8	13/10/1915	13/10/1915
Miscellaneous	77th Infantry Brigade App 8	14/10/1915	14/10/1915
Miscellaneous	77th Infy Bde G. 49 App 9	16/10/1915	16/10/1915
Miscellaneous	A Form Messages And Signals App 10		
Miscellaneous	5th Division G.B. 56/4 App II	17/10/1915	17/10/1915

Type	Description	Start	End
Miscellaneous	15th Infy. Bde. G. 67 App 11	19/10/1915	19/10/1915
Miscellaneous	5th Division. G.B. 56/5 App 12	18/10/1915	18/10/1915
Miscellaneous	15th Infy. Bde. G. 71 App 12	20/10/1915	20/10/1915
Miscellaneous	To HQ 77th Infantry Bde App 13		
Miscellaneous	77th Infantry Brigade App 14		
Miscellaneous	77th Brigade Diary App 15	23/10/1915	23/10/1915
Miscellaneous	11th Scottish Rifles A 16	25/10/1915	25/10/1915
Miscellaneous	A Form Messages And Signals A 16		
Miscellaneous	A Form Messages And Signals App 16		
Miscellaneous	11th Scottish Rifles App 16	25/10/1915	25/10/1915
Diagram etc	Rough Plan Of Position In Front Of 72 73 And 74 Trenches		
Diagram etc	77th Brigade App 16		
Miscellaneous	10th Corps Intelligence Summary App 16	26/10/1915	26/10/1915
Diagram etc	Sub Sector C1 And Pt C2		
Operation(al) Order(s)	5th Division Operation Order No 74 App 18	25/10/1915	25/10/1915
Miscellaneous	77th Infantry Brigade App 17		
Miscellaneous	5th Division G.B. 56/7 A 18	26/10/1915	26/10/1915
Miscellaneous	77th Brigade B.M. 52 A18	26/10/1915	26/10/1915
Miscellaneous	77th Brigade B.M. 70 App 19	27/10/1915	27/10/1915
Miscellaneous	5th Division G.B. 56/8 App 20	28/10/1915	28/10/1915
Miscellaneous	77th Brigade App 20	28/10/1915	28/10/1915
Operation(al) Order(s)	26th Division Order No 9 App 21	27/10/1915	27/10/1915
Miscellaneous	March Table. Moves to take place on 29th and 30th October 1915	30/10/1915	30/10/1915
Miscellaneous	77th Infantry Brigade App 21	28/10/1915	28/10/1915
Miscellaneous	March Table		
Miscellaneous	77th Brigade A 21	29/10/1915	29/10/1915
Miscellaneous	77th Brigade App 22	31/10/1915	31/10/1915
Miscellaneous	Return Shewing Number Of Casualties In 77th Infantry Brigade During Attachment To 5th Division. App 23	01/11/1915	01/11/1915
Heading	26th Division 8th Royal Scots Fusiliers Vol: I Sept. 15 & Oct		
War Diary	Folkestone	20/09/1915	20/09/1915
War Diary	Southampton	20/09/1915	20/09/1915
War Diary	Boulogne	21/09/1915	21/09/1915
War Diary	Saleux	22/09/1915	22/09/1915
War Diary	Fricamps	22/09/1915	23/09/1915
War Diary	Pont De Metz	24/09/1915	24/09/1915
War Diary	Villers Bretonneux	25/09/1915	30/09/1915
Heading	26th Division 8th R.S. Fusiliers Vol: 2 Oct 15		
War Diary	Villers Bretonneux	01/10/1915	05/10/1915
War Diary	Proyart	06/10/1915	18/10/1915
War Diary	Bray	19/10/1915	31/10/1915
Heading	26th Division 10th Black Watch Vol I Sept & Oct. 15		
Miscellaneous	10th (Service) Battn The Black Watch		
War Diary	Sutton Veny Wiltshire	10/09/1915	18/09/1915
War Diary	Havre	19/09/1915	19/09/1915
War Diary	Bougainville	20/09/1915	20/09/1915
War Diary	Sutton Veny	19/09/1915	19/09/1915
War Diary	Shorncliffe	20/09/1915	20/09/1915
War Diary	Boulogne	21/09/1915	21/09/1915
War Diary	Bougainville	21/09/1915	23/09/1915
War Diary	Salouel	24/09/1915	24/09/1915
War Diary	Villers Bretonneux	25/09/1915	29/09/1915
War Diary	Proyart	30/09/1915	30/09/1915

War Diary	Proyart	02/10/1914	02/10/1914
War Diary	Fontaine Les Cappy	02/10/1915	03/10/1915
War Diary	Cappy	03/10/1915	03/10/1915
War Diary	Villers Bretonneux	06/10/1915	11/10/1915
War Diary	Chipilly	12/10/1915	12/10/1915
War Diary	Bray-Sur-Somme	13/10/1915	14/10/1915
War Diary	Carnoy	14/10/1915	17/10/1915
War Diary	Bray-Sur-Somme	18/10/1915	21/10/1915
War Diary	Carnoy	21/10/1915	21/10/1915
War Diary	C, Subsector	21/10/1915	23/10/1915
War Diary	Carnoy C Subsector	24/10/1915	24/10/1915
War Diary	Bray-Sur-Somme	25/10/1915	26/10/1915
War Diary	Etinehem & Chipilly	27/10/1915	29/10/1915
War Diary	Chipilly	30/09/1915	30/09/1915
War Diary	Cardonette	30/09/1915	31/10/1915
Map	Appendix IX		
Map	Appendix II Plan Of Trenches C1 Subsector Carnoy		
Heading	26th Division Cameronians 11th (Scottish Rifles) Vol I Sept 15 & Oct		
Heading	War Diary of 11th Scottish Rifles From September 1st 1915, To September 30th 1915 (Volume 1)		
War Diary	Sutton Veny	01/09/1915	18/09/1915
War Diary	Wilts	18/09/1915	18/09/1915
War Diary	Shorncliffe Camp And Folkestone	19/09/1915	20/09/1915
War Diary	Bouganville Silleux	21/09/1915	24/09/1915
War Diary	Villers Bretonneux	24/09/1915	28/09/1915
War Diary	Cappy	29/09/1915	30/09/1915
War Diary	Moulin	30/09/1915	30/09/1915
Heading	War Diary of 11th Scottish Rifles From October 1st 1915 To October 31st 1915 Volume 2		
War Diary	Moulin Sur Somme	01/10/1915	02/10/1915
War Diary	Cappy	02/10/1915	02/10/1915
War Diary	Villers Bretonneux	03/10/1915	11/10/1915
War Diary	Sally Lorette	12/10/1915	14/10/1915
War Diary	Bray	15/10/1915	17/10/1915
War Diary	B2 Trenches Carnoy	18/10/1915	20/10/1915
War Diary	Bray	21/10/1915	22/10/1915
War Diary	C2 Carnoy	23/10/1915	23/10/1915
War Diary	C2 Trenches Carnoy	24/10/1915	26/10/1915
War Diary	Vaux Sur Somme	27/10/1915	29/10/1915
War Diary	Villers Bocage	30/10/1915	31/10/1915
Miscellaneous	11th Scottish Rifles	25/10/1915	25/10/1915
Miscellaneous	The Officer Commanding, 11th Scottish Rifles	31/10/1915	31/10/1915
Miscellaneous	To Headquarters, 77th Infantry Brigade 2	01/11/1915	01/11/1915
Miscellaneous	The Officer Commanding, 11th Scottish Rifles 3	31/10/1915	31/10/1915
Miscellaneous	From Officer Commanding, 11th The Cameronians (Scottish Rifles) 3	28/10/1915	28/10/1915
Miscellaneous	In Accordance With Your Request, I Have The Honour To Report. As Follows. On The Conduct Of 14,593. Sergeant Meek, 11th Scottish Rifles:-	29/10/1915	29/10/1915
Miscellaneous	77th Brigade 4	31/10/1915	31/10/1915
Heading	26th Division 12th Argylls Vol I Sep 15 & Oct		
War Diary	Sutton Veny	17/09/1915	19/09/1915
War Diary	Boulogne	19/09/1915	21/09/1915
War Diary	St Aubri	22/09/1915	23/09/1915
War Diary	Saleux	24/09/1915	24/09/1915

War Diary	Villers Bretonneux	25/09/1915	25/09/1915
War Diary	Villers Bretonneux	26/09/1915	01/10/1915
War Diary	Villers-Brettux	02/10/1915	02/10/1915
War Diary	Cappy	03/10/1915	06/10/1915
Heading	26th Division 12th Arg & Sutherland Hrs Vol 2 Oct 15		
War Diary	Villers Bretonneux	07/10/1915	12/10/1915
War Diary	Sailly-Lorette	13/10/1915	13/10/1915
War Diary	Bray	14/10/1915	14/10/1915
War Diary	Trenches C2	15/10/1915	17/10/1915
War Diary	Bray	18/10/1915	19/10/1915
War Diary	Trenches C2	20/10/1915	22/10/1915
War Diary	Bray	23/10/1915	25/10/1915
War Diary	Trenches C2	26/10/1915	27/10/1915
War Diary	Bray	28/10/1915	28/10/1915
War Diary	Sailly-Lorette	29/10/1915	29/10/1915
War Diary	Coisy	30/10/1915	31/10/1915

WDSM/2253(1)

WDSM/2253(1)
22.5

26TH DIVISION
77TH INFY BDE

BDE HEADQUARTERS
8TH BN ROY SCOTS FUS.
11TH BN SCOTTISH RIF.
10TH BN BLACK WATCH
12TH BN ARG. & STH. HDRS

SEP - OCT 1915

On His Majesty's Service.

1D/7431

26th Division

HEAD-QUARTERS
77th Inf: Bde.
Vol: 2

SEPT ~ Oct 15

26th Division

Head Quarters
77th Infantry Brigade
Vol. I

Sept. 15

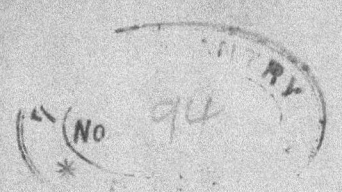

The Adjutant General

    Base.

Herewith War Diary of 77th Brigade up to 30th September, 1915.

4.10.15

                            Brigadier-General

                      Commanding 77th Infantry Brigade

WAR DIARY of the 77th Bde - 26th Division

Army Form C. 2118.

INTELLIGENCE SUMMARY

(Erase heading not required.)

Instructions regarding War Diaries and Intelligence Summaries are contained in F.S. Regs., Part II. and the Staff Manual respectively. Title pages will be prepared in manuscript.

Place	Date	Hour	Summary of Events and Information	Remarks and references to Appendices
Sherrington	Sep 1914		Formed in the early days of September 1914, mainly from newly enlisted men with a proportion of re-enlisted NCOs men - as the 77th Bde of the 26th Division. Composition: 8th R.S. Fusiliers - 11th Scottish Rifles. 10th Black Watch. 12th A & S. 11th Home Station - Sherrington. Sept - November 1914. Bristol Nov 1914 - April 1915. Sutton Veny April - Sept 1915. - Issued with rifles in July 1915.	
Sutton Veny	Sept 1, 1915		Brigade fully mobilized - Br. General Sir H. Stewart Bart Commanding Major J.S. Cunningham Middlesex Regt. Brigade Major Lieut. P. Crenetti General List Staff Captain Captain R.M. Ker A & S Hrs Brigade Machine Gun Officer Lieut. T. Fitz Grant R.S. Bde Signal Officer Lieut. P. Anderson Brigade Grenadier Officer 8th R.S. Fusiliers Lt. Col. H.P. Kerstemen - Bunbury Commanding Major F.F. Buchanan 2nd Command Captain J.A. McGowan Adjutant. Hon Lieut S. Low Quartermaster Strength	

WAR DIARY of 77th Bde 26th Div

INTELLIGENCE SUMMARY.

Army Form C. 2118.

11th Scottish Rifles
Lt. Col. H.H. Thompson Commanding - Major R. Vernon Davidson 2nd in Command
Capt. W. Darby Adjutant. Hon Lt. S.J. Bailey Quartermaster.
Strength

10th Black Watch
Lt. Col. Sir W. Stewart-Dick Cunyngham Bt. Commanding
Major J.H.Y. Livingstone 2nd in Command
Capt. J.C. Sauverson Adjt. N.B. Major C.C. Lamb has been Adjt. up to
the time of embarkation - Was previously Lieut for active service on medical grounds
Hon Lt. J. McLachlan Quartermaster - Strength
12th A.&S. Hrs.

Lt. Col. C.F.H. Davidson Commanding. Major R. Falconer Stewart
2nd in Command - Capt. J.W.S. Miller Adjt. - Hon Lt. J.A. Scott Quartermaster.
Strength -

3/

Army Form C. 2118.

WAR DIARY of 77th Bde 26th Div

INTELLIGENCE SUMMARY.

(Erase heading not required.)

Instructions regarding War Diaries and Intelligence Summaries are contained in F.S. Regs., Part II. and the Staff Manual respectively. Title pages will be prepared in manuscript.

Place	Date	Hour	Summary of Events and Information	Remarks and references to Appendices
Southn. Sutton Vey	Sept 18th		Part of Bde Hdqrs. together with Transport Details of all Bns. left for France travelling via Southampton route.	
Folkestone	19th		Remainder of Hdqrs. & personnel of all Bns. left for France travelling via Folkestone & Boulogne. Owing to expected presence of mines in channel all Bns. delayed 24 hours - bivouacs at Shorncliffe night of 19/20th.	
Boulogne	20th		Bns. crossed & spent remainder of night in rest Camp Boulogne.	
Tricamps	21st & 22nd		Bns. arrived in return by train at Salena marched to Tricamps. Hrs meeting transport details. Hdqrs & 8th R.S.F. Tricamps - 11th S. Rifles & 10. Mach. W. Bn. at Bonqueville 12th A & S.H. St Anton -	
Pont de Metz	23rd		Bns. orders to march to Saleux & hire bivouac - owing to bad weather Brigadier orders to Tillet - which it did as follows 8th R.S.F. 11th S.R. at Pont de Metz. 10th B. Watch & 12. A & S.H. at Saleux	

#353 Wt W3544/1454 700,000 5/15 D.D.&L. A.D.S.S./Forms/C. 2118.

WAR DIARY of 77th Bde 26th Div

Army Form C. 2118.

INTELLIGENCE SUMMARY.
(Erase heading not required.)

Instructions regarding War Diaries and Intelligence Summaries are contained in F.S. Regs., Part II. and the Staff Manual respectively. Title pages will be prepared in manuscript.

Place	Date	Hour	Summary of Events and Information	Remarks and references to Appendices
Villers-Bretonneux	Sept 24th		Billets Villers-Bretonneux	
"	25th		Rest & clean up — All four B'ns received helmets on or abt 26th	
"	26th		Subsequent wearers thrugh own into gas in it. One casualty only leaky helmet, admitted hospital.	
"	27th		Training. Areas allotted	
"	28th		Ditto	
"	29th		11th S. Rifles marched to Cappy thence into trenches for attachment to 80th Bde. 29th Div ain for purpose of instruction. 10th Black Watch marched to PROYART thence into trenches for attachment to 82nd Bde 27th Divisn for purpose of instruction. Other two B'ns training.	
"	30th		11th O. Rifles went into trenches attached to 6th K.R.R. + Rifle Bde. Coy went into trenches, being relieved after 24 hours by other 2 Coys — & so on 10th Black Watch 2 Bn Genl & Bdn. Major attached to Major 80th Bde for instruction	

R.G.F. Ogg Major
A.G. 77th Bde

CONFIDENTIAL.

WAR DIARY

of

77th INFANTRY BRIGADE.

From 1st October 1915 to 31st October 1915

VOLUME II.

Army Form C. 2118.

WAR DIARY of 11th Bn 26th Division

INTELLIGENCE SUMMARY.

(Erase heading not required.)

Instructions regarding War Diaries and Intelligence Summaries are contained in F.S. Regs., Part II and the Staff Manual respectively. Title pages will be prepared in manuscript.

Place	Date	Hour	Summary of Events and Information	Remarks and references to Appendices
Villers-Bretonneux	Oct 1.		11th R. Rifles + 10th Black Watch still in trenches – Other two Bns in Bakers Training. 11th S.R. had 3 casualties. 1 killed + 2 wounded. Two of the casualties were caused by rifle grenade.	
	Oct 2.		B.G. General 113 Bde Major returned to Villers-Bretonneux after attachment to 80th Bde. Major Hay + Major General Mackenzie recced with members of his staff visited part of the line held by 85th Bde – 11th S.R. left trenches at 7.30pm. marched to Hericourt – our Somme where bivouaced. 12th A&S Highrs marched from Villers-Bretonneux to Cappy went into billets. Black Watch in trenches by night – R&Fusiliers Training –	
	Oct 3.		11th S. Rifles marched from Hericourt to Villers-Bretonneux & reoccupied billets – 10th Black Watch still in trenches – 12th A&S H went into trenches attached to K.R.R. Major Bryant 8th Bde 80th Bde R&Fus Training	

WAR DIARY of 77th Bde 26th Division

Army Form C. 2118.

INTELLIGENCE SUMMARY.

(Erase heading not required.)

Place	Date	Hour	Summary of Events and Information	Remarks and references to Appendices
Villers-Brettoneux	Oct 3 Contd		A fire occurred about 10pm in a billet (temporarily vacated by C Coy. 10/Black Watch). The rapid turn out of both Bns (8th R.S.F. & 11/S.R.) in billets & the prompt arrival of the fire piquet of the Scottish Rifles, as the fire was very commendable. The men The Brigade with an aug: we dated 1889 soon arrived. Two other engines from the Station arrived shortly afterwards. The combined efforts of the piquet & firemen prevented the fire spreading, although some furniture & three barns with straw were destroyed before the fire was put out.	
	Oct 4		8th R.S.F. & 11th S.Rifles training. 10th Black Watch marches from Prevost Killieu - Preparations being completed from in the Trenches. 12th Aug. Mr. Churchill in Trenches. Heard that 11 S.R. 770th Black Watch & others on their way they had settled down to has created favourable impression to trench work done in England. trench work. This Christmas Eve tasks in the presence of billets etc. The only really novel condition being ✱	✱ Two men slightly wounded - neither to hospital

Army Form C. 2118.

WAR DIARY 77th Bde 26th Division
or
INTELLIGENCE SUMMARY.

(Erase heading not required.)

Place	Date	Hour	Summary of Events and Information	Remarks and references to Appendices
Villers-Bretonneux	Oct 5		9th R.S. Fusiliers marched to PROYART into hutts for the night for attachment for instructional purposes to 8/12 Bde - 11th S.R. Yrs & 10th BS took both training 12th Aug NCOs recd. Trades Todays tonight into hutts for the night at CAPPY -	
"	Oct 6		12th Aug Higrs returned to hutts at VILLERS - BRETONNEUX after attachment 90th Bde - Casualties 5 wounded. Notification received from Hqrs. 3rd Div. that Bn General School about to be formed will have P. Anderson 10th Black Watch as Chief Instructor & 4 NCOs (1 per Bn) as Asst. Instructors from 9th R.S.F & four NCOs (1 per Bn) & 199th Bdes - 7th MC Division - Others from the 9th S.R & 10th BW training - 8th R&F still in Trenches -	Order Appendix 1.
"	Oct 7		8th R&F still in Trenches - Other Bns in training	
"	Oct 8		Lt Gen Sir H. Wilson KCB MVO Comdg 12th Corps inspected 11th SR. 10th BW 12th Aug NF. Machine Gun Dept & Signallers at training	[signature]

WAR DIARY of 177th Bde 26th Division. Army Form C. 2118.

INTELLIGENCE SUMMARY.
(Erase heading not required.)

Instructions regarding War Diaries and Intelligence Summaries are contained in F. S. Regs., Part II. and the Staff Manual respectively. Title pages will be prepared in manuscript.

Place	Date	Hour	Summary of Events and Information	Remarks and references to Appendices
Villers-Bretonneux	Oct. 9		8th R.S.F. in Trenches. 11th S.R. 10th S.B. 12th Aug. M.G. Training. Lt. Bennett Staff Captain to hospital on medical certificate. Captain C.W. Chinche 11th S. Rifles takes over duties meantime. Bde Major accompanies Lt. Col Maine 8th S.O. of 9th 20th 25th Div to H.Qrs. 5th Division at ETINEHEM. Preliminary Orders to Bde to move into 5th Div: area for a period of 14 days attachment.	APP. 3
			Received from 26th Division — Inlying Picquets 2 Coys A & B 11th turned out & inspected by B.G. General	
—	Oct. 10th		8th R.S.F. returned to Billets in VILLERS-BRETONNEUX for attachment to 81st Brigade at PROYART. Casualties 1 Killed. Orders received from 5th Division for attachment to them. Similar orders received from 26th Division. Massed Pipes & Drums of Bde (less 8th R.S.F) played for ½ of an hour during afternoon in Town Square. Inlying Picquets of Black Watch turned out & inspected by Bgd. General	APP 4. APP 5
	Oct 11th		All Battn's Training. Inlying Picquets of S. Rifles turned out & inspected by B.G.	

2333 Wt. W5544/7454 700,000 5/15 D. D. & L. A.D.S.S./Forms/C. 2118.

Army Form C. 2118.

WAR DIARY of 44th Bde 26th Division

INTELLIGENCE SUMMARY.

(Erase heading not required.)

Place	Date	Hour	Summary of Events and Information	Remarks and references to Appendices
VILLERS-BRETONNEUX	Oct 11 Cont		Major H.S. Buchanan 2nd in Command 9th R.S.F. took over Command of the Bn from Lt Col. H.P. Vans Aminur – Buchanan in accordance with instructions received from H.Qrs. Lt. Col. Buchanan awaiting orders to proceed to England on relinquishing Command.	
SAILLY LORETTE	Oct 12		Bde HQrs, all Bns, 203rd Coy ASC and 1 Sec 90th 4 Ambulance left VILLERS-BRETONNEUX – traveled into billets in 5th Div. Area – distributed as follows night of 12th/13th. Bde HQrs SAILLY LORETTE – 9th R.S.F. VAUX-SUR-SOMME, N.H.S. Rifles & 12th A&S Hy. SAILLY LORETTE 10th B.Watch & Seafs. & Aust. CHIPILLY – 203rd Coy ASC parked near SAILLY-le-Sec.	APP. 6.
— " —	Oct 13		10th B. Watch. & 12th A&S Hy. moved into billets at BRAY & came under Command of 13th & 15th Bdes respectively. – Bde HQrs to have Bn remain as for 12th inst. Sea.fs & Aust no longer under Command 77/Bde but attached 5th Div. Bt General Robb Major Haitz Hqrs 157Bde, visited various Bn HQrs including HQrs Dorset Regt. and Bn rifle Arra Luck now situated.	APP 7
— " —	Oct 14		Bt General visited 9th R.S.F. at VAUX – 10th Black Watch & 12th A&S Hy moved into Kennels night 14/15th & took over a Bn sector of trench line of 13th & 15th Bdes respectively. HQrs & other Bn remain as for 12th inst.	APP 7A (15th Bn only)

WAR DIARY

Army Form C. 2118.

of 10 / K Bn 77 / 26 Division

INTELLIGENCE SUMMARY.

(Erase heading not required.)

Place	Date	Hour	Summary of Events and Information	Remarks and references to Appendices
BRAY	6.9.18		Bn HQrs moved from SAILLY LORETTE to BRAY - Bn moved from VAUX and SAILLY LORETTE respectively, went into trenches in BRAY. - 10th Black t 12th aug 17s in trenches, having relieved Staffords, KOYLI & Highland Regt respectively. 8.30 pm night 4/5th Report received as follows. Relief of 11 Cheshire Regt by 12th Aug 17s had just taken place, some of the Cheshire not having left the trenches. When Germans opened rapid fire on our trenches. This was followed by the explosion of two mines immediately afterwards. Three fixed mortar bombs were fired also shells from field guns. - About 50 yards of the front trench was blocked & part of a communicating trench. Minus had a few casualties. All the A & B Bn were evacuated & there was no hospital cases. - Regular Officers attached to the Bn for instruction spoke afterwards of the excellent way in which Lt Speir & Ld 2/Lt of B Coy (Capt Peirse) k'd A Coy in the explosion to tell of the 1/k has behaved. This particularly referred to B Coy (Capt Peirse) in whose section the explosion occurred. - On subsequent examination the explosion (which formed a considerable crater) appears to have taken place immediately in front & not under our trench with the result that the trench was blown in rather sideways than up. - After the explosion nothing further were greatly rammed by the Officers & the clearing & repair of the trench proceeded with.	APP. 8
"	6.9.18		8th RSF & 11th SR in BRAY. 10th BW & 12th AE 8ths in trenches 13th BW Qu nails HQrs Brieuls Cas SThs Bertrancourt & Boulogne 15th BW vector Wellington Redoubt & Machine Gun Positions in work near Harp Dorset Regt Minden Post	

Army Form C. 2118.

WAR DIARY of 9th Bn. 26th Division

or

INTELLIGENCE SUMMARY.

(Erase heading not required.)

Instructions regarding War Diaries and Intelligence
Summaries are contained in F. S. Regs., Part II.
and the Staff Manual respectively. Title pages
will be prepared in manuscript.

Place	Date	Hour	Summary of Events and Information	Remarks and references to Appendices
BRAY	Oct 19		8th R.S.F. moves from Billets Bray into Trenches C1 Sector (15th Bde) 11th S.R. to Billets to Trenches B Sector (13th Bde) 10th Black Watch to Trenches B Sector to Billets BRAY - 12th A&S.M. Trenches C Sector to Billets BRAY. Casualties during 3 days Black Watch 2 officers wounded, 3 Killed other ? wounded. A&S M.G. 3 wounded. Conditions in trenches normal.	APP 9 (15th Bde only)
"	Oct 19		As above - Quiet day, certain amount of firing at night from 2am 19th - 6am. mostly enemy Machine Guns 9.0.E 26th S.R. noted to trenches -	
"	Oct 19		Same as 19th - 9.0.E. 8th Bde wired trenches. 12th A&S M.G. manned position in subsidiary line during darkness - 7-18th	APP 10
"	Oct 20		8th R.S.F. in trenches 11 S.R. from trenches B Sector to Billets BRAY to under 13th Bde. Casualties during tour 2 men killed 1 wounded. 10th Black Watch Billets 12th A&S M.G. Billets to Trenches C 2.	APP 11
"	Oct 21		8th R.S.F. Trenches C1 to Billets BRAY - 11th S.R. remain Billets BRAY - 10.B.W. Billets BRAY to Trenches C1 - 12 A&S M.G. in Trenches - 77th Bde Hqrs now to Hqrs 15th Bde and 9.0.E 77th Bde assumes command of C Sector - Casualties 1 wounded	APP 12
"	Oct 22		6/10/ 12 noon Quiet night - 11 S.R. manned position in subsidiary line during darkness. Batn in weather per Ren.	
"	Oct 23		8th R.S.F Billets BRAY. 11th S.R. Billets to Trenches C2 Subsection. 10th B.W. in Trenches 12th A&S M.G. Billets BRAY from Trenches C2 - Just before relief of A & S M by	APP 13 APP 14

WAR DIARY of 77th Bde 26th Division

INTELLIGENCE SUMMARY.

(Erase heading not required.)

Army Form C. 2118.

Instructions regarding War Diaries and Intelligence Summaries are contained in F. S. Regs., Part II. and the Staff Manual respectively. Title pages will be prepared in manuscript.

Place	Date	Hour	Summary of Events and Information	Remarks and references to Appendices
Bray	Oct 23		11th SR in C2. Officer of Tunnelling Co. reported that Germans have completed mine to left of Crater opposite Trench 73. Mine apparently between enemy trench from —	
	Oct 24		8th R/RSF relieved 10th B.W. in Trenches C1. – B.W. to huts – 11 S.R. in trenches. 12th A&S Hrs in huts. –	APP 15.
	Oct 25		Sgt HAMETZ at 2 am Enemy exploded a mine opposite Trench 73 in Sussects C2 occupied by the 11th SR. The mine made a crater judged to be 75 yds by 50 yds and about 30 feet deep. Considerable damage was done to the parapet of 73 & part of 74 – also a spread of proportion of 72 & 73 trenches was blown in – The explosion was expected & repairs were begun at once. Bomb bombers under Lt Thurburn Cheshire Reg. & Lt Brangsfield 11th SR occupied the new crater which is being connected with our trench. Casualties see appendix. The Adjutant of the 11th SR was excellent throughout. Our artillery shelled German sap & crater showing aptitude from —	APP 16
			9th R.SF in Trenches – 10th B.W. & 12th A&S Hrs in huts	
	Oct 26		8th R/RSF in trenches. 12th A&S Hrs relieved 11th SR in Subsects C2 10th B.W. in huts. — Enemy shells BRAY-FRICOURT road – 1 man wounded. 10th B.W. marched to trench to entrain which the Army are sending to Newchurch Railway on fatigues. Two lorries from 5 pm to 12 midn. A.D.S.S./Forms/C. 2118 each to Newchurch Railway on fatigues. —	APP 17

WAR DIARY of 77th Bde. 26 Division

INTELLIGENCE SUMMARY

Army Form C. 2118.

Place	Date	Hour	Summary of Events and Information	Remarks and references to Appendices
BRAY	Oct 27		8th R.S.F in Trenches. 12th Cas 8th in Trenches. On beginning stretch by 15th Bde 11 S.R. move from BRAY to bluffs in VAUX-SUR-SOMME and 10th R.S.U. from BRAY to ETINGHEM & CHIPILLY during relief in BRAY by 1st Regt & Kampfr. Regt respectively.	APP 18
	Oct 28		8th R.S.F + 12th Cas8th relieved in Trenches C2 + C1 by 15th Bde - went u/r with BRAY.	APP 19
SAILLY LORETTE	Oct 29		8th R.S.F + 12th Cas8th moved to billets SAILLY LORETTE - & Seela moved one to G.O.C. 15th Bde. - Br. General Sir H. H. Steward handed over command of 77th Inf. Bde to Bt Col Hibbert D.S.O. - Br. Gen. Steward left for England. Bde H.Qrs moved to SAILLY LORETTE.	APP 20
VILLIERS BOCAGE	Oct 30		Bde marches from 5th Div. Area into 2nd Div Area - Bn in marching from 15 - 20 miles. March discipline. Appearance of the Bn. - Small numbers falling out was very satisfactory. Lt. Gen Holland watches the Bde march through QUERRIEUX. Billets & much Harn + MSR VILLERS BOCAGE. 8th R.S.F at RAINNEVILLE - 10th Black Watch CARDONNETTE 12th Cas 8th at COISY	APP 21

WAR DIARY 82. 77th Bde 26th Division
INTELLIGENCE SUMMARY.

Place	Date	Hour	Summary of Events and Information	Remarks and references to Appendices
VILLERS BOCAGE	Oct 31st		Bns in billets. Conference of Commanding Officers in forenoon. Congratulatory orders received. Casualties during period of attachment to 51st Division	APP 22 APP 23

Lieut Colonel
Cmdg 77th Bde

APP. 78.

7th Brigade.
78th do.

Copy to "C".
 "   to 12th Corps.
 "   to 27th Division.
 "   to 78th Brigade.

In substitution of my No. G.78, dated 29.9.1915, your instruction in trench warfare will be carried out in accordance with attached programme.

Battalions will march to MERICOURT SUR SOMME and arrive there at 2.30 p.m., one Officer from each Battalion reporting to 27th Division Headquarters at that place 15 minutes before the arrival of the Battalion for guides.

Billeting parties on bicycles will move one hour ahead of Battalion and report to 27th Divisional Headquarters.

R.b Hare

1.10.1915.
                                            Lieut. Colonel,
                                    General Staff, 26th Division.

APP 1

G.78.

Attachment of 77th and 79th Brigades.

Date.	80th Brigade at CAPPY.	82nd Brigade at PROYART.
Sept.30th.	10th Black Watch in the trenches.	11th Scottish Rifles in the trenches("A" and "B" Coys.)
Oct. 1st.	do.	do.
Oct. 2nd.	10th Black Watch return to Hd. Qrs. 12th A. & S. Hdrs. march to CAPPY with Brigade Machine Guns, less those of R.Scots Fusiliers.	do ("C" & "D" Coys.)
Oct. 3rd.	Argyll & Suth. Hrs. in trenches.	do.
Oct. 4th.	do.	11th Scottish Rifles return to H.Q. 8th Rl. Scots. Fus. march to PROYART with machine guns.
Oct. 5th.	Argyll & Suth.Hrs. return to H.Q. No. 1 Batt.,79th Bde., marches to CAPPY.	~~11th Scottish Rifles return to~~ 8th R.Scots. Fusiliers in trenches "A" and "B" Companies
Oct. 6th.	No. 1 Batt., 79th Bde., in trenches.	do.
Oct. 7th.	do.	8th Rl.Scots.Fus. in trenches ("C" and "D" Coys.)
Oct. 8th.	No. 1 Batt., 79th Bde., return to H.Q. No. 3 Batt., 79th Bde., march to CAPPY.	do.
Oct. 9th.	No. 3 Batt., 79th Bde.in trenches.	R.Scots.Fus. return to H.Q. No. 2 Batt., 79th Bde., march PROYART.
Oct.10th.	do.	No. 2 Batt., 79th Bde. in the trenches ("A" & "B" Coys.)
Oct. 11th.	No. 3 Batt.79th Bde.return to H.Q. No. 4 Batt.79th Bde. march to CAPPY.	do.
Oct.12th.	No.4 Batt.79th Bde. in trenches.	do.("C" & "D" Coys
Oct.13th.	do.	do.
Oct.14th.	No.4 Batt.79thBde. return to H.Q.	No. 2 Batt.79th Bde., return H.Q.

26th Div. No. G/78.

77th Infantry Brigade.
~~79th Infantry Brigade.~~

1. Reference my G/78 dated 1/10/15, 10th Black Watch have been attached to the 82nd Brigade at PROYART and the 11th Scottish Rifles to the 80th Brigade at CAPPY, consequently the 11th Scottish Rifles are coming out of the trenches today and the 10th Black Watch on 4th instant. The 12th Argyll and Sutherland Highlanders will relieve the 11th Scottish Rifles.

2. The R.Scots Fusiliers will not move into the trenches from PROYART until the 6th inst. and consequently will not march out till the 5th instant.

No.2 Batt, 79th Brigade, will move to PROYART on the 10th instant, returning on the 15th instant.

.... Major,
for Lieut.Colonel,
General Staff, 26th Division.

2/10/15.

APPENDIX 2

"A" Form.   Army Form C. 2121.

MESSAGES AND SIGNALS.   No. of Message

TO: 77th Brigade

Sender's Number: G.185 Day of Month: 6/10   AAA

A grenade school will shortly be formed at VILLERS BRETONNEUX with Lieut. ANDERSON 10th Black Watch as Chief Instructor aaa The following officers will be required to act as assistant Instructors Lieut MCOWAN 8th R.S.F. Lieut WICKS 7th O.B.L.I. Lieut PECK 10th Devons aaa Two NCOs per Brigade will also be required as assistant Instructors aaa These NCOs should be selected from those who have done well during recent course in bombing aaa Names to be submitted by 6 pm 7th instant

From: 25th Division
Time: 7.45 pm

APPENDIX 3

SECRET

To "A"
G.O.C.
77th Infantry Brigade.
~~26th Signal Company.~~

1. On Tuesday, October 12th, the 77th Infantry Brigade will move into the 5th Divisional area for a period of 14 days attachment.

2. Billeting parties will meet a representative from the Q. Staff, 5th Division, at the Church at SAILLY - LORETTE at 11 a.m.

3. Brigade Headquarters will be established at SAILLY--LORETTE in the first instance.

4. The 203rd Company of the Divisional Train will accompany the 77th Brigade and will come under the orders of the G.O.C. 5th Division.

Refers to 'A' Branch only

5. Supply and Medical arrangements will necessitate consultation with the Q. Branch, 5th Division, with whom you should correspond early.

P.V. Hac

9/10/15.

Lieut. Colonel,
General Staff, 26th Division.

APP. 4

SECRET.

5th Division Operation Order No. 72.

10th October, 1915.

1. The 77th Infantry Brigade and 203rd Train Company from 26th Division, are to be attached to the 5th Division from the 12th instant for about 14 days.
    They will be billeted on night 12th/13th in CHIPILLY, SAILLY LORETTE and VAUX.
    Billeting parties will meet a representative of the Administrative Staff, 5th Division, at SAILLY LORETTE Church at 11 a.m. on 12th instant.
    G.O.C. 77th Infantry Brigade will report the arrival of his troops in the 5th Division area, and will then come under the command of the 5th Division.

2. The 77th Infantry Brigade and 203rd Train Company are being attached to the 5th Division for the purpose of gaining experience in the ordinary routine of trench warfare.
    The 203rd Train Company will be attached to the 5th Divisional Train.
    The 77th Infantry Brigade Signal Section will be attached to the 5th Divisional Signal Company.
    The 77th Infantry Brigade has already done eight days in trenches for training as platoons and companies.
    The training with the 5th Division will be divided into two periods.
    During the first period, two battalions (A and C) will be attached to the 13th Infantry Brigade, and two battalions (B and D) to the 15th Infantry Brigade.
    During the first period each battalion will be allotted a battalion sub-sector to hold for three days, in accordance with attached table.
    Two battalions each of 13th and 15th Infantry Brigades will be withdrawn into reserve on the arrival of the battalions of the 77th Infantry Brigade, and will form, for purposes of command, a composite brigade under Lt.Colonel C.R.J.Griffith, C.M.G., D.S.O., 1st Bedf. Regt.
    Battalions of 13th, 15th and 77th Infantry Brigades will continue to be administered and rationed by their own Brigades throughout.
    During the second period, the 77th Infantry Brigade will hold 'C' Sector of the 5th Division front, and the 15th Infantry Brigade (less 6th Liverpool Regt.) will be withdrawn into the reserve area.

3. In order that the battalions of the 77th Infantry Brigade may gain experience from more seasoned troops, G.O.C's 13th and 15th Infantry Brigades will arrange to attach to a battalion of the 77th Infantry Brigade holding a sub-sector of their front, the adjutant, transport officer and quartermaster sergeant, and one officer per company, of the battalions being replaced in that sub-sector.
    O.C. 5th Divisional Signal Company will, during the first period of attachment, distribute the 77th Infantry Brigade Signal Section amongst the three Brigade Sectors. During the second period of attachment, he will
    allot

Operation Order No. 72 (continued).

        allot the 77th Infantry Brigade Signal Section, as a unit, to a Brigade sector other than 'C' Sector.

    4.   Table of moves is attached. G.O.C. 77th Infantry Brigade will report which battalions correspond to the letters A, B, C and D, given in the table.
        Further details for the moves on the 13th/14th, 15th/16th, 20th/21st and 21st/22nd, will be issued.

    5.   ACKNOWLEDGE.

                                              Lt.Colonel,
                        General Staff, 5th Division.

Issued at 8 a.m.

    Copies to :-

        10th Corps.
        12th Corps.
        26th Division.
        13th Inf. Bde.
        14th   "   "
        15th   "   "
        77th   "   "
        5th Division 'Q'.
        C.R.A.
        C.R.E.
        Div. Squadron.
        Div. Cyclist Co.
        Divisional Train.
        A.D.M.S.
        5th Signal Co.
        S.S.O.
        D.O.O.

APP 4

TABLE of MOVES - (Issued with 5th Division Operation Order No. 72.

Date	Unit	From	To	Remarks.
12th October.	77th Inf. Bde. 203rd Train Co.	26th Div. area	CHIPILLY, SAILLY Lorette and VAUX.	Come under command of 5th Div. on arrival. A Battn. to CHIPILLY, B and C Battns. to SAILLY LORETTE, D Battn. to VAUX.
Oct.13th/14th.	A Battn. 77th I.Bde. B " " " 1 Battn. 13th I.Bde. 1 " 15th " "	CHIPILLY SAILLY LORETTE BRAY or BRONFAY BRAY	BRAY or BRONFAY BRAY SAILLY LORETTE ETINEHEM and CHIPILLY.	Comes under command of 13th Inf. Bde. on arrival. Comes under command of 15th Inf. Bde. on arrival. Comes under command of 77th I.Bde. For work on intermediate line. Comes under command of 77th I.Bde
Oct.14th/15th.	A Battn. 77th I.Bde. B " " " 1 " 13th " " 1 " 15th " "	BRAY or BRONFAY BRAY Trenches Trenches	Trenches B Sector. " C " BRAY or BRONFAY. BRAY	
Oct.15th/16th.	C Battn 77th I.Bde. D " " " Bde. H.Q. " "	SAILLY LORETTE VAUX SAILLY LORETTE	BRAY or BRONFAY. BRAY BRAY	Comes under command of 13th Bde. " " " 15th " To be attached to 15th Bde. Lt.Col.C.R.J.Griffith CMG DSO to command composite bde. in reserve area.
	1 Battn. 13th I.Bde. 1 " 15th " "	BRAY or BRONFAY BRAY	SAILLY LORETTE VAUX	
Oct.17th/18th.	A Battn. 77th I.Bde. B " " " C " " " D " " "	Trenches B Sector " C " BRAY or BRONFAY BRAY	BRAY or BRONFAY. BRAY Trenches B Sector " C "	

Table of Moves (continued).

Date	Unit	From	To	Remarks.
Oct. 20th/21st	1 Battn. 13th I.Bde.	SAILLY LORETTE	Trenches B Sector	A double shift can be made if preferred.
	C " 77th "	Trenches B Sector	BRAY	To 15th Bde. area and comes under command of 15th I.Bde.
	1 " 15th "	BRAY	SAILLY LORETTE	
	B " 77th "	BRAY	Trenches C Sector	
	1 " 15th "	Trenches C Sector	BRAY	
Oct. 21st/22nd.	A " 77th "	BRAY (13th Bde. area)	Trenches C Sector	Comes under command of 15th Bde.
	D " " "	Trenches C Sector	BRAY	
	1 " 13th "	SAILLY LORETTE	BRAY	
	1 " 15th "	BRAY	SAILLY LORETTE	
	15th Bde. H.Q.	BRAY	SAILLY LORETTE	G.O.C. 77th I.Bde. takes over command of C Sector on completion of relief of D Battn by A Battn.

APP 4

5th Division.
G.B. 58/1.

13th Inf. Bde.
15th "   "
77th "   "

1. With reference to first sentence of para. 3 of 5th Division Operation Order No. 72, the detail of Officers and N.C.O's laid down to be attached to battalions of 77th Infantry Brigade, need only be regarded as a guide, and need not be exactly followed.

G.O.C's 13th and 15th Infantry Brigades will attach such Officers and N.C.O"s to battalions of 77th Infantry Brigade as seem most likely to be useful to the latter, and should G.O.C. 77th Infantry Brigade desire it, will arrange for Officers and N.C.O's of 77th Infantry Brigade to be attached to their battalions.

2. On completion of attachment of 10th Black Watch and 11th Scottish Rifles to 13th Infantry Brigade, and transfer to 15th Infantry Brigade, Officers and N.C.O's of 13th Infantry Brigade attached to those battalions will be withdrawn, and will be replaced by Officers and N.C.O's from 15th Infantry Brigade.

5th Division,					Lt.Colonel,
11/10/15.				General Staff, 5th Division.

77th Infantry Brigade Copy No 1.
APP 5

SECRET.

Extract from 5th Division Operation Order No. 72.
----

1. The 77th Infantry Brigade and 203rd Company Train from 26th Division, are to be attached to the 5th Division from the 12th inst. for about 14 days.
    They will be billeted on night 12th/13th in CHIPILLY--SAILLY LORETTE and VAUX.
    Billeting parties will meet a representative of the Administrative Staff, 5th Division, at SAILLY LORETTE Church at 11 a.m. on 12th instant.
    G.O.C. 77th Infantry Brigade will report the arrival of his troops in the 5th Division area, and will then come under the command of the 5th Division.

2. The 77th Infantry Brigade and 203rd Train Company are being attached to the 5th Division for the purpose of gaining experience in the ordinary routine of trench warfare.
    The 203rd Train Company will be attached to the 5th Divisional Train.
    The 77th Infantry Brigade Signal Section will be attached to the 5th Divisional Signal Company.
    The training with the 5th Division will be divided into two periods.
    During the first period, two battalions, 10th Black Watch and 11th Scottish Rifles will be attached to the 13th Infantry Brigade and two battalions, 12th Argyll and Sutherland Highlanders and 8th Royal Scots Fusiliers, to the 15th Infantry Brigade.
    During the first period each battalion will be allotted a battalion sub-sector to hold for three days, in accordance with the attached table.
    Two battalions each of 13th and 15th Infantry Brigades will be withdrawn into reserve on the arrival of the battalions of the 77th Infantry Brigade, and will form, for purposes of command, a composite Brigade under Lt. Colonel C.R.J.Griffith, C.M.G., D.S.O., 1st Bedf. Regt.

    Battalions of 13th, 15th and 77th Infantry Brigades will continue to be administered and rationed by their own Brigades throughout.
    During the second period, the 77th Infantry Brigade will hold 'C' Sector of the 5th Division front, and the 15th Infantry Brigade (less 6th Liverpool Regt.) will be withdrawn into the reserve area.

3. In order that the battalions of the 77th Infantry Brigade may gain experience from more seasoned troops, G.O.C's 13th and 15th Infantry Brigades will arrange to attach a battalion of the 77th Infantry Brigade holding a sub-sector of their front, the adjutant, transport officer and quartermaster sergeant, and one officer per company, of the battalions being replaced in that sub-sector.
    O.C. 5th Divisional Signal Company will, during the first period of attachment, distribute the 77th Infantry Brigade Signal Section amongst the three Brigade Sectors. During the second period of attachment, he will allot the 77th Infantry Brigade Signal Section, as a Unit, to a Brigade sector, other than 'C' Sector.

4. Further details for the moves on the 13th/14th, 15/16th, 20th/21st and 21st/22nd, will be issued later.

App 5

TABLE OF MOVES. (Issued with 5th Division Operation Order No. 72.)

Dates.	Unit.	From.	To.	Remarks.
12th October.	77th Infantry Brigade. 203rd Train Co.	26th Div. Area.	CHIPILLY, SAILLY LORETTE and VAUX.	Come under command of 5th Div. on arrival. 10th Black Watch, 12th to CHIPILLY, 12th A. and S. Hrs. and 11th Scottish Rifles to SAILLY LORETTE, 8th R.Scots. Fusrs. to VAUX.
Oct.13th/14th.	10th Black Watch, 77th Infy. Bde.	CHIPILLY.	BRAY or BRONFAY.	Comes under command of 13th Inf. Bde. on arrival.
	12th A. & S. Hrs. do.	SAILLY LORETTE.	BRAY.	Comes under command of 15th Inf. Bde. on arrival.
	1 Battn. 13th do.	BRAY or BRONFAY.	SAILLY LORETTE. ETINEHEM and CHIPILLY.	Comes under command of 77th Inf. Bde. For work on intermediate lines. Comes under command of 77th Infy. Bde.
	1 Battn. 15th do.	BRAY.		
Oct.14th/15th.	10th Black Watch, 77th Infy. Bde	BRAY or BRONFAY.	Trenches B Sector.	
	12th A.& S.Hrs. do.	BRAY.	" C "	
	1 Battn. 13th do.	Trenches.	BRAY or BRONFAY.	
	1 Battn. 15th do.	Trenches.	BRAY.	
Oct. 15th/16th.	11th Scot.Rifles. 77th Infy. Bde.	SAILLY LORETTE.	BRAY or BRONFAY.	Comes under command of 13th Bde.
	8th Rl. Scots. Fus. do.	VAUX.	BRAY.	do. 15th "
	Bde. Hd. Qrs. do.	SAILLY LORETTE.	BRAY.	To be attached to 15th Bde. Lieut. Col. C.R.J. Griffith, C.M.G. D.S.O., to command composite Bde in reserve area
	1 Battn. 13th Infy. Bde.	BRAY or BRONFAY.	SAILLY LORETTE.	
	1 " 15th "	BRAY.	VAUX.	

5th Div. Order No. 72 (Moves, continued).

Date.	Unit.	From.	To.	Remarks.
Oct.17th/18th.	10th Black Watch, 77th Infy. Bde. 12th A.& S. Hrs. do. 11th Scot.Rifles. do. 8th Rl.Scots.Fus. do.	Trenches,B.Sector. " C. " BRAY or BRONFAY. BRAY.	BRAY or BRONFAY. BRAY. Trenches, B.Sector. " C. Sector.	
Oct. 20th/21st.	1 Battn. 13th Infy. Brigade. 11th Scot.Rifles,77th Infy. Bde. 1 Battalion, 15th do. 12th A.& S. Hrs.77th do. 1 Battalion, 15th do.	SAILLY LORETTE. Trenches,B.Sector. BRAY. BRAY. Trenches,C.Sector.	Trenches, B. Sector. BRAY. SAILLY LORETTE. Trenches, C.Sector. BRAY.	A double shift can be made if preferred. To 15th Bde. area and comes under command of 15th In.Bde.
Oct. 21st/22nd.	10th Black Watch, 77th Infy. Bde. 8th Rl.Scots.Fus. do. 1 Battn. 13th. do. 1 Battn. 15th do. 15th Bde. Hd. Qrs.	BRAY (13th Bde.area Trenches,C.Sector. SAILLY LORETTE. BRAY. BRAY.	Trenches,C. Sector. BRAY. BRAY. SAILLY LORETTE. SAILLY LORETTE.	Comes under command of 15th Bde. G.O.C. 77th Infy. Bde. takes over command of C. Sector on completion of relief of 8th Rl. Scots. Fusrs. by 10th Black Watch.

12

APP 5   APP 6

MOVE ORDERS   77th BRIGADE   COPY No.

Reference Amiens Sheet No. 12.

1. Move Orders C 3 of last night are cancelled and the following substituted.

2. Brigade Hdqrs, All Battalions, 203rd Coy A.S.C., 1 Section 80th Field Ambulance will move independently into billets 5th Division Area on 12th instant, in accordance with March Table.

3. <u>March Table</u>

Unit	S. Point	Time	Route	Billets	Time of Arrival of Head of Unit at Billets
8/R.S.F.	Rue de POUILLY at a pt due W of pt 104	2.20 pm	FOUILLOY CORBIE	VAUX SUR SOMME	4.10 pm
10/B.W.	Cross Rds 400X N of S in VILLERS BRETONNEUX	12.30 pm	WARFUSEE - ABANCOURT - road leading N past pt 66 - SAILLY LORETTE	CHIPILLY	3.30 pm
Bde Hdqrs Sig Sec	do	1.15 pm	WARFUSEE - ABANCOURT	SAILLY LORETTE	3.25 pm
12/A.&S.H.	do	1.20 pm	- road leading N post pt 66		3.30 pm
11/B.R.	do	1.50 pm	do	do	4 pm
203rd Coy A.S.C.	do	12 noon	Same as Black Watch	Parked about ½ mile S W of SAILLY LE SEC	2.30 pm
Sec 80th F.A.	do	8.30 a.m.	Route as per Black Watch	CHIPILLY	12 noon

4. Billeting Parties, on bicycles, from all units, will report to Staff Captain 9.30 a.m. outside Bde Hdqrs, 12th instant, and will then proceed to SAILLY LORETTE CHURCH.

Transport
    5. Transport, including train wagons, will accompany units.

        Refilling Point 12th instant same place as before 7.30 am—

        13th instant, at point 108 due N of first S in SAILLY LE SEC

        All units will send supply wagons empty from new billets

        on 12 instant to a point about ½ a mile S.W. of SAILLY-LE-

        SEC where 203rd Coy will be parked.

Ammunition
    6. S. A. A. Carts will be taken filled.

    7. Notified for information that Brigade Headquarters will

        be at SAILLY LORETTE night 12/13th.

    8. O. C. Units will report arrival in Billets to Brigade

        Headquarters.

Salvage Company
    9. All N.C.O.s and men medically unfit but exclusive of

        those in hospital will be attached to Division Salvage

        Company. Arrangements to be made direct with O. C.

        Salvage Company.

Copies No. 2 to 5th Division.

    No. 3 to 26th Division.

    No. 4 to 8th Royal Scots Fusiliers.

    No. 5 to 11th Scottish Rifles.

    No. 6 to 10th Black Watch.

    No. 7 to 12th Argyll & Sutherland Highrs.

    No. 8 to 203rd Coy. A.S.C.

    No. 9 to 80th Field Ambulance.

                                        Major.

11.10.15.   Brigade Major 77th Infantry Brigade.

APP 7

44th Bde.   Battery (Coy No 1)

BM 283

Movement of troops on 13th inst. will be as follows:-

1. Billeting parties of 10. B.W. and 12th A + S. H'rs will move as under.

B.W. from CHIPILLY. New transport Hdqrs 13th Bde BRAY at 12 noon.

A. S. H'rs from SAILLY LORETTE 10.45 am to report Hdqrs 15th Bde BRAY 12 noon.

2. A + S. H'rs and B.W. will move as under:—

Unit	S.P.	Time	Route	Billets	Remarks
12th A+S.H'rs	Billets Sailly Lorette	4.20 pm	Pt 105 on BRAY-CORBIE Rd — pt 80 (little west of BRAY)	BRAY	Heads of B'ns will not pass pt 80 before 6 pm
10th B.W.	Billets Chipilly	5.35 pm	WESTERN EDGE of ETINEHEM — pt 80	BRAY	Head of B'ns will not pass pt 80 before 6.45 pm

3. Arrival of B'ns at new billets to be reported to Bde. Hdqrs at once.

4. 8th R.S.F. & 11.S.R. will remain at VAUX sur SOMME & SAILLY LORETTE respectively.

5. Bde HQrs remains at SAILLY LORETTE.
6. Acknowledge.

12.10.15.

Munozka
Major
Adj Major 77/Bde.

Copy No 2 to 5th Div.
3 to 26th Bde.
4 to 8th RSF
5 to 11th SR
6 to 1st BW
7 to 12 A&S Hrs
8 to Sec: SO & O.
9 to 203rd Coy.

APP 7 APP 7

5th Division.
G.B. 56

Movement of troops on the 13th will be as follows :-

1. Billeting parties of 10th Black Watch and 12th Argyle and Sutherland Highrs. will report at 13th and 15th Infantry Brigade Headquarters BRAY, at 12 noon.

2. 12th Argyle and Sutherland Highrs. will march from SAILLY LORETTE to BRAY via Point 105 on BRAY - CORBIE road. March to be timed so as to reach Point 80, 1 mile west of BRAY, at 6 p.m., and that point is not to be passed before that hour.

3. The battalion of 13th Infantry Brigade marching to SAILLY LORETTE will march so as to reach Point 80 at 6 p.m.

4. 10th Black Watch from CHIPILLY will march via western edge of ETINEHEM and point 80. March to be timed so as to reach point 80 at 6.45 p.m.

5. The battalion of 15th Infantry Brigade marching to ETINEHEM and CHIPILLY, to march via ETINEHEM. Battalion to reach road junction immediately west of BRAY at 6 p.m.

6. A.P.M. will arrange road control between point 80 and the Town Hall BRAY between 6 p.m. and 7 p.m.

7. Arrival of battalions to be reported to Divisional Headquarters by G.O.C's Brigades.

8. Acknowledge.

                                                Lt.Colonel,

11.10.1915.   General Staff, 5th Division.

Copies to

5th Division 'Q'.
G.R.A.
A.P.M.
13th Inf. Bde.
15th "   "
77th "   "
Div. Train

13ʰ

APP 7A

TABLE OF MOVES (ISSUED WITH 15th INF. BDE. OPERATION ORDER No 10)

Date	Unit	From	To	Remarks
13th/14th Oct	"B" Battalion 15th Inf Bde	SAILLY LORETTE	BRAY	Comes under Command of 14th Inf Bde on arrival
	1st Bedford Regt.	BRAY	"ETINEHEM" and CHIPILLY	Comes under command of 14th Inf Bde
14th/15th Oct	"D" Battalion 15th Inf Bde @ 12" A a8 15th 1st Cheshire Regt	BRAY Trenches Subsector C2	Trenches Subsector C2 BRAY	
15th/16th Oct	"D" Battalion 15th Inf Bde Bde H.Q. 15th Inf Bde 1st Norfolk Regt.	VAUX SAILLY LORETTE BRAY	BRAY BRAY VAUX	Comes under Command of 15th Inf Bde. To be attached to 15th Inf Bde. Lt Col C.R.J. Griffith C.M.G. M.S.O. to Command temporarily in reserve area
17th/18th Oct	"D" Battalion 15th Inf Bde 1st Cheshire Regt. "D" Battalion 15th Inf Bde 1st Dorset Regt.	Trenches Subsector C2 BRAY BRAY Trenches Subsector C1	BRAY Trenches Subsector C2 Trenches Subsector C1 BRAY	
20th/21st Oct	1st Dorset Regt "B" Battalion 15th Inf Bde 1st Cheshire Regt	BRAY BRAY Trenches Subsector C2	SAILLY LORETTE Trenches Subsector C2 BRAY	
21st/22nd Oct	"B" Battalion 15th Inf Bde "D" Battalion 15th Inf Bde 1st Cheshire Regt 15th Bde H.Q.	BRAY (Wood Bivouac) Trenches Subsector C1 BRAY BRAY	Trenches Subsector C1 BRAY SAILLY LORETTE SAILLY LORETTE	Comes under command of 15th Inf Bde. G.O.C. 14th Inf Bde takes over Command of C Sector on completion of relief of "D" Battalion by 1st Battalion

APP 7A

15th Bde Orders

APP 8

5th Division.
G.B. 56/2.

Moves on 15th instant will be as follows :-

i. Billeting parties of 11th Scottish Rifles and 8th Royal Scots Fusiliers to report at 13th Infantry Brigade and 15th Infantry Brigade Headquarters at BRAY respectively, at 12 noon.

ii. Battalion of 15th Infantry Brigade marching to VAUX to reach Point 80 on BRAY - CORBIE road at 5.45 p.m.

iii. Battalion of 13th Infantry Brigade marching to SAILLY LORETTE to reach Point 80 on BRAY - CORBIE road at 6.15 p.m.

iv. Battalion of 77th Infantry Brigade marching from SAILLY LORETTE to BRAY to reach Point 105 on BRAY - CORBIE road at 5.15 p.m.

v. Battalion of 77th Infantry Brigade marching from VAUX to BRAY to reach Point 105 on BRAY - CORBIE road at 5.45 p.m.

vi. A.P.M. to arrange road control between Points 80 and 105 between 5.15 p.m. and 6.45 p.m.

ACKNOWLEDGE.

5th Division,
13/10/1915.

A.A. Cameron   Lt.Colonel,
General Staff, 5th Division.

Copies to :-

5th Division 'Q'.
C.R.A.
13th Inf. Bde.
14th "   "
15th "   "
77th "   "
Div. Train
A.P.M.
A.D.M.S.
S.S.O.

Bray BM 324 APP 8

MOVE ORDERS 77th Infantry Brigade. Copy No. 8

1. The 11th Scottish Rifles and 8th Royal Scots Fusiliers will move into Billets at BRAY tomorrow 15th instant and will come under command of 13th and 15th Brigades respectively.

2. March Table.

Unit	S.P.	Time.	Route	Remarks.
11th S.Rifles	Billets Sailly Lorette	4.20 p.m.	pt.105 pt.80	To reach pt. 105 at 5.15 p.m.
8th R.S.Fus:	Billets Vaux.	4.15 p.m.	Bray Corbie Road pts 108 105-80.	To reach pt. 105 at 5.45 p.m.

3. Billeting parties of the 11th Scottish Rifles and 8th Royal Scots Fusiliers will report at 13th Infantry Brigade and 15th Infantry Brigade Headquarters at BRAY respectively at 12 noon 15th instant.

4. Brigade Headquarters will be at BRAY from 12 noon tomorrow and will be attached to Headquarters 15th Brigade.

5. All Battalions on arriving at BRAY will send baggage wagons to 203rd Coy. Army Service Corps unless required for storage purposes in which case a report will be made to this office. In any case the horses, harness and drivers will be sent.

 Major.

14.10.15. Brigade Major 77th Infantry Brigade.

Copies to 5th Division.
 26th Division.
 8th Royal Scots Fusiliers.
 11th Scottish Rifles.
 10th Black Watch.
 12th A. & S. Highrs.

203rd Coy ASC 8.

App 9

15th Infy. Bde.
G. 49.

77th Infy. Bde.

1. In accordance with Operation Order No.10, the following reliefs will take place to-morrow night 17th/18th October:-

    (a) 8th Royal Scots Fusiliers will relieve 1st Dorset Regt. in C.1 Subsector.

    (b) 1st Cheshire Regt. will relieve 12th Argyll and Sutherland Highlanders in C.2 Subsector.

2. All details regarding reliefs will be settled by Battalion Commanders concerned, with following limitations:-

    (a) No troops or vehicles will leave BRAY before 5.15 p.m.

    (b) 1st Cheshire Regt will lead followed by 8th R.Scots Fusiliers whose Companies will march at 5 minutes interval. The 2 Companies 8th R.Scots Fusiliers for right of Subsector will move via BRONFAY FARM where guides will meet them; the two Companies for left of Subsector by Railway Loop, guides meeting them at point where railway crosses road (F 28b 2/5).
    No guides will be required for 1st Cheshire Regt.

    (c) Company Commanders, Grenadier Officer and Machine Gun Officer of 8th Royal Scots Fusiliers will go into position in daylight and will meet incoming troops on arrival in trenches. Telephone operators will also be sent in advance.

3. On relief 1st Dorset Regt. and 12th Argyll and Sutherland Highlanders will withdraw to BRAY, taking over respectively billets vacated by 8th R.Scots Fusiliers and 1st Cheshire Regt.

4. O.C. 8th Royal Scots Fusiliers will send 2 S.A.A. Limbers to CARNOY to replace S.A.A. Carts of 1st Dorset Regt.

5. Completion of reliefs will be reported to Brigade Headquarters.

    ACKNOWLEDGE.

[signature]
Captain,
Brigade Major, 15th Inf.Bde.

16th October, 1915.

Copies to-
  1st Cheshire Regt.
  1st Dorset Regt.
  8th R.Scots Fusiliers.
  12th A. & S. Highrs.
  5th Division.
  77th Infy. Brigade.

"A" Form.
MESSAGES AND SIGNALS.
Army Form C. 2121.

APP 10

Prefix	Code	m.	Words	Charge	This message is on a/c of:	Recd. at	m.
Office of Origin and Service Instructions			Sent			Date	
			At	m.		From	
			To		Service.	By	
			By		(Signature of "Franking Officer.")		

TO : (15th Bde.) 19th Bde.

Sender's Number	Day of Month	In reply to Number		AAA
ASH/63	18th	—		

Test	S 14	aaa	Orders	received
5·35 pm	looking	Coy	left	6·5 p.m.
Batt Hd-Qrs	arrived	at	SUBSIDIARY	TRENCHES
6·56 pm	aaa	Two	Coys [A+B]	in
SUBSIDIARY	TRENCHES	with	position	with
2 Machine-guns	7·0 p.m.	C. Coy	in	position
in	LUCKNOW	REDOUBT	with	1 Machine Gun
7·20 p.m.	D Coy	in	position	WELLINGTON
REDOUBT.	7·25. p.m.	aaa.	Pack	mules
with	LUCKNOW	REDOUBT	Coy.	aaa.
2S97	carts	to	Batt Hd-Qrs.	aaa.
Or-Mr	and	Transport Off.	warned	of
dispositions.	aaa.	Stragglers	were	sent
out	and	arrived	at	SUBSIDIARY
TRENCH	7·20 p.m.	aaa.	1 Machine-Gun	to
L4c 5/6	at	7. p.m.		

From 12th Argylls.
Place
Time

The above may be forwarded as now corrected.   (Z) E. Mills Capt + adjt A&SH
Censor.   Signature of Addressor or person authorised to telegraph in his name.

<u>5th Division.</u>
G.B. 56/4

Movements on the 20th October will be as follows :-

1. Billeting party of 11th Scottish Rifles will report at 15th Infantry Brigade Headquarters at 12 noon.

2. Detachment 2nd K.O.S.B. moving from ETINEHEM to the trenches will be clear of the western end of BRAY by 5.45 p.m.

3. Battalion of 15th Infantry Brigade marching to SAILLY LORETTE will move as soon as road is clear of 2nd Bn. K.O.S.B.

4. 11th Scottish Rifles on relief will move into the 15th Inf. Bde. area in BRAY.

17/10/1915.

A.R. Cannon
Lt.Colonel,
General Staff, 5th Division.

Copies to -

5th Division 'Q'.
13th Infantry Bde.
14th   - do -
15th   - do -
77th   - do -

15th Infy. Bde.
G. 67.

<u>77th Inf. Bde.</u>

The following relief and movements will take place to-morrow night 20th/21st October, 1915:-

1. 12th Argyll and Sutherland Highlanders will relieve 1st Cheshire Regt. in Subsector C.2.
All details regarding relief will be settled by Battalion Commanders concerned. No guides will be required. No troops or vehicles will leave BRAY before 5.15 p.m.

2. On relief 1st Cheshire Regt. will withdraw to billets at BRAY.

3. 1st Cheshire Regt. will take over mining fatigues from 12th Argyll and Sutherland Highlanders from relief commencing at 1.30 a.m. on 21st October, 1915.

4. 1st Dorset Regt. marching to SAILLY LORETTE will move as soon as road is clear of detachment of 2nd K.O.S.B. moving from ETINEHEM to trenches. This detachment has been ordered to be clear of the Western end of BRAY by 5.45 p.m.

5. 11th Scottish Rifles on relief from trenches in 13th Inf. Bde. area will move into the 15th Inf. Bde. area in BRAY.

6. Completion of relief and movements will be reported to Brigade Headquarters.

ACKNOWLEDGE.

A H Ransome
Captain,

19th October, 1915.   Brigade Major, 15th Inf. Bde.

Copies to -
    1st Cheshire Regt.
    1st Dorset Regt.
    12th A. & S. Highlanders.
    8th R. Scots Fusiliers.
    11th Scottish Rifles.
    5th Division.
    77th Infy. Brigade.

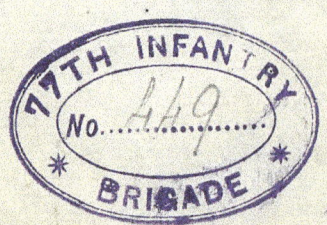

APP 12

13th Inf: Bde.
14th "   "
15th "   "
77th "   "
5th Div: "Q"

5th Division. G.B.

56/5

Detail of movements for evening of October 21st will be as follows:-

(1)　O.C. 10th Black Watch to report himself at 15th Bde. Headquarters on the morning of 20th instant, to receive orders regarding occupation of "Q" 1. Sub-sector on night 21st/22nd.

(2)　The 10th Black Watch come under orders of 15th Inf: Brigade at 5.p.m. on 21st instant.

(3)　Battalion of 15th Brigade marching from BRAY to SAILLY-LORETTE and Battalion of 13th Brigade marching from SAILLY-LORETTE to BRAY to march so as to pass one another at point 80 at 5.45.p.m.

5th Division.　　　　　　A.R.Cameron　　　　　Lt Colonel.
18.10.15.　　　　　　　General Staff, 5th Division.

77TH INFANTRY BRIGADE No. 435

Acknowledged 15.4.
no copy in book

Communicated to
O.C. Black Watch

15th Infy. Bde.
G. 71.

77th Infy. Bde.

The following relief and movements will take place on the night 21st/22nd October:-

1. 10th Black Watch will relieve 8th R.Scots Fusiliers in C.1 Subsector.

2. All details regarding relief will be settled by Battalion Commanders concerned with the following limitations:-
    (a) No troops or vehicles are to leave BRAY before 5.15 p.m.
    (b) The two Companies for right of subsector will move via BRONFAY Farm where guides will meet them.
        The two Companies for left of subsector will move via road through L 9d, L 10a, L 4c, L 4a, to Railway Loop, guides meeting them at point where railway crosses road F 28b 2/5.
        O.C. R.Scots Fusiliers will detail above guides and will also provide guides for machine guns.
    (c) Company Commanders, Grenadier Officer and Machine Gun Officer will go into position in daylight and will meet incoming troops on arrival in trenches. Telephone operators will also be sent in advance.

3. On relief 8th R.Scots Fusiliers will withdraw to billets at BRAY.

4. O.C. 10th Black Watch will send 3 S.A.A. Limbers to CARNOY to replace those of 8th R.Scots Fusiliers.

5. 1st Cheshire Regt. marching from BRAY to SAILLY LORETTE will march so as to pass Battalion of 13th Inf. Bde. marching from SAILLY LORETTE at point 80 on BRAY - CORBIE road at 5.45 p.m.

6. Orders as regards mining fatigues have been issued separately.

7. On completion of relief of 8th R.Scots Fusiliers, 15th Infantry Brigade Headquarters will move to SAILLY LORETTE.

ACKNOWLEDGE.

Captain,
Brigade Major, 15th Inf. Bde.

20th October, 1915.

Copies to -
  1st Cheshire Regt.
  8th R.Scots Fusiliers.
  10th Black Watch.
  12th A.& S. Highlanders.
  11th Scottish Rifles.
  77th Infantry Brigade.
  5th Division.

APP 9B 3

To HQ 77th Infantry Bde

1. In accordance with verbal orders from Bde Major at 5·15 pm tonight — I left my Billets at 6pm to reinforce the A & S Highlanders.

2. The Company for WELLINGTON REDOUBT reported to the Officer in charge at 7.13 pm
   Lucknow Redoubt at 7pm and the 2 Coys south of CITADEL, with machine guns were in position at 7pm

3. The Battⁿ returned to Billets at 8.10 pm

H A Thompson Lt Col

8·15pm 22/10/15

Bray

APP 14

B.M. 462

77th Infantry Brigade.

The following relief and movements will take place tomorrow night 23/24th October 1915.

1. 11th Scottish Rifles will relieve 12th Argyll & Sutherland Highrs in subsector C 2.

All details regarding relief will be settled by Battalion Commanders concerned with following limitations.

(a) No troops or vehicles to leave Bray before 5.15 p.m.

(b) Company Commanders, Grenadier Officer and Machine Gun Officer will go into position by daylight and meet incoming troops on arrival in trenches.

Telephone operators will also be sent in advance.

Guides will not be required.

2. Following trench stores will be handed over to relieving Battalion:

All S.A.A. dumped in trenches and Battalion Headquarters.

All grenades and very ammunition   ---"---

Vermorel sprayers.   Hysto syringes.

Fire proof clothing   35 sets.

Rum jars.

Periscopes other than box pattern and ordinary trench stores.

Following stores will not be handed over:

Knob Kerries - Telescopic sights - Box periscopes - range finders - Picks & Shovels - Very Pistols.

3. 11th Scottish Rifles will arrange to keep 4 full S.A.A. carts, without horses at the Citadel.

4. On completion of relief O.C. Battalions concerned will forward to this office a return showing number of boxes S.A.A. ammunition - grenades, trench stores etc. handed over and taken over respectively.

5. On relief the 12th Argyll & Sutherland Highrs will take over billets vacated by 11th Scottish Rifles on N side of Rue Corbie.

6. 12th Argyll & Sutherland Highrs will take over daily mining fatigues from 11th Scottish Rifles as follows from 1.30 a.m. 24th October.

Bricourt centre   1.30 a.m. - 7.30 a.m.   20 men
                       7.30 a.m. - 12.30 p.m.   "
                       12.30 p.m. - 7.30 p.m.   "
                       7.30 p.m. & 1.30 a.m.   "

Fatigues under an Officer and proportion of N.C.O.s will parade at Citadel F 21 d 5/8 at above hours.

7. Completion of relief and movements will be reported to Brigade Headquarters.

Acknowledge.

                                      Major.

Copies to

8th Royal Scots Fusiliers.   Brigade Major 77th Infantry Bde.
11th Scottish Rifles.
10th Black Watch.
12th Argyll & Sutherland Highrs.
5th Division.
26th Division.

22nd Brigade. Diary APP 15
B.M.6.

The following relief and movements will take place on the night 24/25th October 1915.

1. 8th Royal Scots Fusiliers will relieve 10th Black Watch in C.1.Subsector.

2. All details regarding relief will be settled by Battalion Commanders concerned with following limitations:-

(a) No troops or vehicles to leave Bray before 5.15 p.m.

(b) The two Companies for right of subsector will move via BRONFAY FARM where guides will meet them. The two Companies for left of subsector will move via road through L 9d, L 10a, L 4c, L 4a to railway loop guides meeting them at point where railway crosses road F 28b 2/5

(c) Machine Guns & Telephone Operators to be sent in advance of Companies.

2. O.C. 10th Black Watch will detail above guides, also guides for Machine Guns, time and place for latter to be arranged by O.C. Battalions.

3. 8th Royal Scots Fusiliers wille send 3 S.A.A. limbers full to Carnoy to replace those of 10th Black Watch.

4. On relief 10th Black Watch will move into billets in BRAY vacated by 8th Royal Scots Fusiliers.

5. 10th Black Watch will take over daily mining fatigues from 8th Royal Scots Fusiliers.

    1.30 a.m. - 7.30 a.m.   30 men.
    7.30 a.m. - 12.30 p.m.   "
    1.30 p.m. - 7.30 p.m.   "

The above fatigues under an officer and proportion of N.C.O.s will parade at citadel at times stated.

6. Completion of Reliefs to be reported to Brigade Headquarters.

Acknowledge.

signature
Major.

23.10.15.   Brigade Major 77th Infantry Brigade.

Copies to
8th Royal Scots Fusiliers.
11th Scottish Rifles.
10th Black Watch.
12th A. & S. Highrs.
5th Division.
26th Division.

11th Scottish Rifles
A. 16

Report of enemy mining
operations on morning of
25.10.15

C 2 Sector

About 1.45 a.m. an enemy mine was exploded on the right of 73 Trench; at the same time a sap head of ours was destroyed on the left of 72 Trench.

a Stokes shell is said to have been fired

The explosion was accompanied by a heavy shell and rifle fire.

A new CRATER was formed in front of the right of 73 Trench. This was occupied by the Brigade Grenadier Officer and 2nd Lieut. Dangerfield of this Regt, with about 10 regimental Bombers. They held the whole of the new CRATER, until dawn. As it was found the enemy's old CRATER enfiladed the new one. Major

Davidson (who was in command) decided to withdraw them.

The enemy made no attempt to occupy the new CRATER.

The damage done to our trenches was as follows:—

(a) 40 yards of no 73 trench parapet driven in.

(b) Practically the remaining parapet of 73 will have to be rebuilt, as the explosion drove the parapet back at least a foot.

(c) 60 yards of no 74 Trench requires repairing.

Casualties — One Officer Scottish Rifles was wounded in the wrist whilst rebuilding parapet. No men were injured by explosion of mine; but the following casualties occurred in the Sap, already mentioned.

        Killed
1   R.E.
3   Q.V. Rifles
—
4

        Wounded
5. Scottish Rifles ⎫
3   Q.V. Rifles   ⎬ gassed & injured
2   R.E.   ⎭
—
10

Artillery. The Observing Officer reported himself to me at 2.15 a.m. I asked him to fire 8 rounds to protect my working party.

Action taken. The O.C. in command of N°2 Co (73) Trench reported to me at 2.10 a.m. of the explosion. I directed him to clear away the damaged parapet, and at the same time, sent him one

platoon from my Support with
sand bags, picks and shovels
to assist him.

It was impossible to
sap out to the new CRATER
until the debris of the parapet
and listening posts had been
cleared:

Reports | Report of mine explosion sent to
Bde HQ and to Royal Fusiliers
and Scots Fusiliers

Proposed action } | Repairing fire trenches in 73
and 74.
Sapping out to new CRATER.
Constructing and repairing old
Listening Posts.

10 am
25/10/15

H A Morrison Lt Col
Comm'g 9 11th Scottish Rifles

"A" Form. Army Form C. 2121.
MESSAGES AND SIGNALS.
No. of Message A/16

Prefix	Code	m.	Words	Charge	This message is on a/c of:	Recd. at	m.
Office of Origin and Service Instructions.			Sent			Date	
			At	m.	Service.	From	
			To				
			By		(Signature of "Franking Officer.")	By	

TO — HQ 77th Inf Bde

| Sender's Number | Day of Month | In reply to Number | AAA |
| SRR 532 | Twenty fifth | | |

Report of enemy's mining operations this morning forwarded herewith

From: Commanding 11th Scottish Rifles
Place: C2
Time: 10 am

The above may be forwarded as now corrected.

Censor.   (Z) HA Thompson Lt Col
Signature of Addresser or person authorised to telegraph in his name

* This line should be erased if not required.

"A" Form.
MESSAGES AND SIGNALS.

Army Form C. 2121.

No. of Message **APP 1b**

Prefix	Code	m.	Words	Charge	This message is on a/c of:	Recd. at	m.
Office of Origin and Service Instructions.			Sent			Date	
			At ... m.		.... Service.	From	
			To				
			By		(Signature of "Franking Officer.")	By	

TO 5th Division

Sender's Number	Day of Month	In reply to Number	
BM 33	25		AAA

Situation report aaa at 2 a.m. enemy exploded mine opposite 73 trench destroying unknown length of parapet and blowing in saphead on left of 72 trench aaa explosion expected repair parties were ready and quickly started repairs aaa Our bombers occupy new crater aaa trench is being constructed to connect crater with our trench aaa Our bombers have bombed crater during night aaa Position is now normal aaa Work light casualty aaa Casualties red star two gassed four of whom miners aaa One Officer wounded repairing trench Added 5th Div repeated 13th & 15th Bde.

From 77 Bde
Place
Time 5.35 a.m.

Manninghe
Major
77 Bde

App 16

11th Scottish Rifles.

Report of enemys mining operations on morning of 25/10/15.

C 2.
Sector.   About 1.45 a.m. an enemy's mine was exploded on the right of 73 Trench; at the same time a sap head of ours was destroyed on the left of 72 Trench.

The explosion was accompanied by a heavy shell and rifle fire.   A Stink shell is said to have been fired.

A new CRATER was formed in front of the right of 73 Trench. This was occupied by the Brigade Grenadier Officer and 2/Lieut Dangerfield of this regiment, with about 10 regimental bombers.   They held the whole of the new crater until dawn, as it was found the enemy's old CRATER enfiladed the new one.   Major. Davidson (who was in command) decided to withdraw them.

The enemy made no attempt to occupy the new crater.

The damage done to our trenches was as follows:-

(a) 40 yards of No. 73 trench parapet driven in.

(b) Practically the remaining parapet of 73 will have to be rebuilt, as the explosion drove the parapet back at least a foot.

(c) 60 yards of No. 74 Trench requires repairing.

Casualties   One Officer, Scottish Rifles was wounded in the wrist whilst rebuilding parapet.   No men were injured by explosion of mine: but the following casualties occurred in the sap, already mentioned.

Killed.

1 R. E.
3 Q. V. Rifles.

Wounded.

5 Scottish Rifles.)
3 Q. V. Rifles.   ) gassed and
2 R. E.   ) injured.

Artillery.   The observing Officer reported himself to me at 2.15 a.m. I asked him to fire 8 rounds to protect my working party.

APP 16

Action Taken.
The O. C. in Command of No. 2 Coy. (73) Trench reported to me at 2.10.am. of the explosion. I directed him to clear away the damaged parapet, and at the same time sent him one platoon from my support with sandbags, picks and shovels to assist him.

It was impossible to sap out to the new crater until the debris of the parapet and Listening posts had been cleared.

Reports
Reports of mine explosion sent to Brigade Headquarters and to Royal Fusiliers and Scots Fusiliers.

Proposed Action.
Repairing fire trench in 73 and 74.
Sapping out to new crater. Constructing and repairing old Listening posts.

10 a.m.
25/10/15.

H. A. Thompson. Lt. Colonel.
Commanding 11th Scottish Rifles.

Headquarters,
    5th Division.

Herewith copy of report made by O.C. 11th Scottish Rifles on explosion of mine this morning.

Also rough plan indicating what the present position is considered to be. It will be noticed that the report says the mine was exploded on the right of 73 trench - whereas the sketch shows it left of 73.

My Brigade Major accompanied Col. Thompson round the position this morning, and as far as one can tell crater appears to be pretty well in front of 73.

Hugh H Stewart
Brigadier-General.

25/10/15.
Commanding 77th Infantry Brigade.

APP 16

Rough plan of positions in front of
72 73 and 74 Trenches

Drany

APP 16

77th Brigade.

Situation Report as regards C 2 is now as follows:-

Parapet of Trenches 73 & 74 have been to all intents and purposes repaired although there is still work to be done.

As regards the new crater it has been found inadvisable to occupy our side because it is commanded by enemy's side.

The following rough sketch will explain what is being done and proposed.

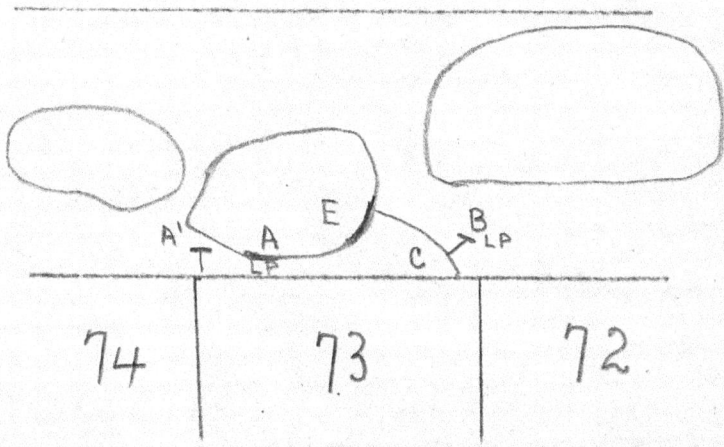

A is listening post on the edge of crater in existence. Sentry crawls out through what is the remains of part of the old D for about 20 yards to A¹ (Sandbag parapet) then turns right to listening post.

B is listening post in existence.

C is remains of D loop and is being cleared out with the idea of making a trench at E which will be it is considered at least in as good a position as any trench the Germans may make on their side.

Yesterday the Artillery bombarded the German side of the crater and claim to have reduced the height considerably. Colonel Thompson is of opinion that the guns damaged the trenches constructed on the edges of the old craters a good deal.

Wire has been erected right end of 74.

Menninghe Major.

26.10.15.   Brigade Major 77th Infantry Brigade.

No. 58.   26th October, 1915.

10th CORPS INTELLIGENCE SUMMARY.

OPERATIONS.

    NORTHERN DIVISION. Our Trench Mortar battery replying to enemy's trench mortars got a direct hit on the mound at R.31.c.2.3. Splintered timber was seen protruding from the top of the mound.

    CENTRE DIVISION. Enemy blew up small mine at 5.15 a.m. on 24th in F.10.b., no material damage was done. West Guns and rifle grenades were used with effect in D. Sector on 24th. Enemy exploded a mine in F.10.c.7.4 on night of 24th/25th. We sapped out to the crater and are joining sap head to our lines. Enemy have been active with grenades in F.9.d.8.7 and we replied with rifle grenades and West Guns. We sucessfully exploded a mine opposite LA BOISSELLE at 1 p.m. on 25th. German machine guns were busier than usual last night. We dispersed German working parties near FRICOURT with grenades and machine gun fire.

    SOUTHERN DIVISION. Enemy exploded a mine at 2 a.m. on 25th South of MAMETZ. A sap head was blown in and some parapet was destroyed; the explosion was expected and repairs were started at once. Our bombers occupied the new crater which is being connected with our trench.

INTELLIGENCE.

    NORTHERN DIVISION. Sounds of mining reported opposite THIEPVAL salient at R.25.a.5.0.

    CENTRE DIVISION. At 3.30 p.m. on 24th a working party was seen carrying beams from X.20.d.6.1. to X.20.d.8.2.

    SOUTHERN DIVISION. Enemy displayed a white flag near MARICOURT WOOD bearing the words "ZUTRITT VERBOTEN" (Admission forbidden). Enemy's snipers were less active opposite A Sector yesterday.

DISTRIBUTION OF ENEMY'S FORCES.

    XIV Reserve Corps. According to an official document the 216th Feld-Maschinengewehr-Zug (3 guns) is with the 119th Reserve Regt.

    XVII Corps. Authentic documents confirm the presence in France of the 61st Regt., 35th Division on 15th October, and of the 5th Grenadier Regt., 36th Division on 17th October. Both divisions are in the area West of ST QUENTIN.
    There is reason to believe that a force of about one division moved by rail through MONS and VALENCIENNES between the 16th and 19th October. It appeared to have come from Germany.

ENEMIES CASUALTIES. The following casualties are reported for the 1st and 2nd Bns., 157th Regt., 117th Division in the 359th Prussian Casualty List published on 21st October, 1915 :-

	Killed.	Wounded.	Prisoners.	Missing.	Total.
Officers (including acting officers).	-	1	-	25	26
N.C.Os (including Lance Corporals)	17	13	-	176	206
Men	39	111	-	978	1128
TOTALS =	56	125	-	1179	

/These

These are the first casualties of the 157th Regt., reported for the LOOS fighting which began on 25th September. The casualties of the 3rd Bn. have not yet appeared.

XV Corps. The following casualties are reported in the 358th and 359th Prussian Lists published on the 20th and 21st October 1915 for the 172nd Regt. :-

	Killed.	Wounded.	Missing.	Prisoners.	Total.
Officers (including acting officers).	9	7	2	-	18
N.C.Os (including lance Corporals)	36	79	43	-	158
Men	131	366	181	1	679
TOTALS =	176	452	226	1	855

These were presumably suffered during the British attack South of the YPRES - MENIN road on 25th September. The casualties of the 126th Regt. XV Corps and of the 246th and 248th Reserve Regts. 54th Res. Division, XXVII Res. Corps have not yet appeared.

VII Corps. The following casualties are reported in the 359th Prussian List, published on 21st October, 1915 for the 11th Jager Bn. :-

	Killed.	Wounded.	Suffering from gas poisoning.	Prisoners.	Missing.	Total.
Officers (including acting officers)	3	3	-	-	-	6
N.C.Os (including lance corporals)	12	26	3	-	-	41
Men	51	129	2	-	-	182
TOTALS-	66	158	5	-	-	229

This is the first time that casualties from gas poisoning have been reported.

The above casualties were apparently suffered in the fighting South of the LA BASSEE Canal on 25th September.

GENERAL

DUMMY MORTAR BATTERIES WITH SMOKE RINGS.

A captured German order of the 2nd Bavarian Foot Artillery Bde. dated 1st August states that experiments which have been made with a view of getting rid of the ring of smoke produced when a mortar is fired have not given satisfactory results.

An attempt has consequently been made to produce this ring artificially in dummy batteries. The apparatus used is a cylindro-conical tin tube 1 m. 90 cm. long and 40 cm. in diameter in the cylindrical part which is charged with 150 grams of black powder. It is placed at the entrance of the shelter holding the men that work it.

The smoke is produced on receipt of a telephone message from the battery or on hearing the mortar fire.

It is said to work excellently.

SHIELDS IN TRENCHES.

The following is a translation of an order issued by the

VIII Res. Corps on 23rd July 1915. :-

/"The

APP 16

Sub Sector C.1
and ½ C2

CARNOY
FRANCIS AVENUE

APP

Scale 1/5000

Relief

APP 18

5th Division Operation Order No. 74.

25th October, 1915.

1. On completion of its tour of instruction in the trenches 77th Infantry Brigade will be relieved by 15th Infantry Brigade in 'C' Sector and will withdraw into the Reserve Brigade area together with 203rd Train Company.

2. Relief will be carried out as follows :-

    October 27th/28th. 1st Bn. Norfolk Regt. from VAUX and 1st Bn. Bedford Regt. from CHIPILLY and ETINEHEM will move into Brigade reserve in BRAY.

    11th Bn. Scottish Rifles and 10th Black Watch will withdraw to VAUX and CHIPILLY (and ETINEHEM) respectively.

    October 28th/29th. 1st Bn. Bedford Regt. and 1st Bn. Norfolk Regt. will relieve 8th R.S.Fusiliers and 12th A. & S.Highrs. in 'C' Sector trenches respectively, the latter battalions withdrawing into Brigade Reserve in BRAY.

    October 29th/30th. 1st Bn.Dorset Regt. and 1st Bn.Cheshire Regt. from SAILLY LORETTE will move into Brigade Reserve in BRAY.

    8th R.S.Fusiliers and 12th A. & S.Highrs. will withdraw into Reserve Area at SAILLY LORETTE.

3. When the relief on night 29th/30th is completed, G.O.C. 15th Infantry Brigade will take over command of 'C' Sector from G.O.C. 77th Infantry Brigade, the latter taking over command of his own Brigade in the Reserve area.

4. On October 30th, the 77th Infantry Brigade will come under orders of 26th Division.

5. ACKNOWLEDGE.

Lieutenant Colonel,
General Staff, 5th Division.

Copies to:-
10th Corps.	26th Division.
13th I.Bde.	5th Division 'Q'.
14th ,,	C.R.A.
15th ,,	C.R.E.
77th ,,	Div.Squadron.
A.D.M.S.	Signal Co.
S.S.O.	Div.Cyclist Co.
D.O.O.	Divisional Train.

APP 17

77th Infantry Brigade.

B.M. 43.

The following relief and movements will take place tomorrow night 26/27th October 1915.

12th Argyll & Sutherland Highrs will relieve 11th Scottish Rifles in subsector C 2.

All details regarding relief will be settled by Battalion Commanders concerned with following limitations.

(a) No troops or vehicles to leave Bray before 5.15 p.m.

(b) Company Commanders, Grenadier Officer and Machine Gun Officer will go into position by daylight and meet incoming troops on arrival in trenches.

Telephone operators will also be sent in advance.

Guides will ~~not~~ be required. as before.

2. Following trench stores will be handed over to relieving Battalion:

All S.A.A. dumped in trenches and Battalion Headquarters.

All Grenades and very ammunition ---"---

Vermorel Sprayers.   Hysto syringes.

Fire proof clothing 35 sets.

Rum jars.

Periscopes other than box pattern and ordinary trench stores.

Following stores will not be handed over:

Knob Kerries - Telescopic sights - Box periscopes - range finders - Picks & Shovels - Very Pistols.

3. 12th Argyll & Sutherland Highrs will arrange to keep 4 full S.A.A. Carts, without horses at the Citadel.

4. On completion of relief O.C. Battalions concerned will forward to this office a return showing number of boxes S.A.A. ammunition - grenades, trench stores etc. handed over and taken over respectively.

APP 17

5. On relief the 11th Scottish Rifles will take over billets vacated by 12th Argyll & Sutherland Highrs on N side of Rue Corbie.

6. Orders for mining fatigues will be issued later.

7. Completion of relief and movements will be reported to Brigade Headquarters.

Acknowledge.

Major.

Brigade Major 77th Infantry Brigade.

Copies to

8th Royal Scots Fusiliers.
11th Scottish Rifles.
10th Black Watch.
12th Argyll & Sutherland Highrs.
5th Division.
26th Division.

5th Division.
G.B. 56/7

Movements of troops on the 27th instant will be as follows :-

1. 1st Norfolk Regt. will march from VAUX to BRAY via Point 105 on BRAY - CORBIE Road. March to be timed so as to reach Point 80, one mile west of BRAY, at 5 p.m., and that point is not to be passed before that hour.

2. 1st Bedford Regt. will march via western edge of ETINEHEM and Point 80 to BRAY. March to be timed so as to reach Point 80 at 5.45 p.m.

3. 10th Black Watch to march to ETINEHEM and CHIPILLY via ETINEHEM. Battalion to reach road junction immediately west of BRAY at 5 p.m.

4. 11th Scottish Rifles marching to VAUX will march so as to reach Point 80 at 5 p.m.

5. Billeting parties will report at noon as follows :-

    i. Those of battalions of 77th Inf. Bde. to battalions of 15th Inf. Bde. with which they are exchanging, and

    ii. Those of 1st Norfolk and 1st Bedford Regts. to Staff Captain 77th Inf. Bde.

6. A.P.M. will arrange road control between Point 80 and the Town Hall BRAY between 5 and 6 p.m.

7. Arrival of battalions to be reported to Divisional H.Q. by G.O.C's Brigades.

8. Acknowledge.

5th Division,
26th Oct., 1915.

Lt.Colonel,
General Staff, 5th Division.

Copies to -

    13th Inf. Bde.
    15th "   "
    77th "   "
    C.R.A.
    Q.

MOVE Bray   77th BRIGADE.   B.M. 52.   A18

1. Details of movements of troops on 27th instant will be in accordance with March Table.

March Table.

Unit	S.P.	Time	Route	Billets	Remarks.
11th S.R.	pt.80	5.p.m.	pts 105 108 cross roads N E of Vaux.	Vaux sur Somme.	Relieve 1st Norfolk Regiment.
10th B.W.	road junction immediately W of BRAY	5 p.m.	L 20 A Etinehem	Chipilly and Etinehem.	Relieve 1st Bedford Regiment.

2. Billeting parties will report as under/27th noon

   11th Scottish Rifles to Headquarters 1st Norfolk Regt. Vaux.

   10th Black Watch to Headquarters 1st Bedford Regt. Chipilly.

3. Arrival in billets of Battalions to be reported by O.C. Battalions to G.O.C. 15th Brigade, Sailly Lorette under whose orders they will then come until 77th Brigade Headquarters moves to Sailly Lorette evening of 29th.

4. Pipes and Drums will not play on high ground E of MEAULTE - ETINEHEM Rd.

5. Road control out of Bray is arranged by A.P.M. 5th Division.

6. Refilling Point as hitherto.

Acknowledge

                         Major.

26.10.15.   Brigade Major 77th Infantry Brigade.

Copies to 8th Royal Scots Fusiliers, 11th Scottish Rifles, 10th Black Watch, 12th A. & S. Highrs., 203rd Coy. A.S.C., 15th Brigade, 5th Division, 26th Division.

Draft

77th Brigade   B. M. 78.

A.P.P 19

The following relief and movements will take place on night 28th/29th October 1915.

1. 1st Bedford Regt. will relieve 8th Royal Scots Fusiliers in subsector C^1 and 1st Norfolk Regt. the 12th Argyll & Sutherland Highrs in subsector C^2.

2. All details concerning reliefs to be settled by O. C. Battalions concerned subject to the following limitations:
(a) No troops or vehicles to leave BRAY before 5.15 p.m.

3. 1st Bedford Regt. will replace 3 S.A.A. Carts of 8th Royal Scots Fusiliers at Carnoy and 1st Norfolk Regt. 4 S.A.A. Carts of 12th Argyll & Sutherland Highrs at CITADEL.

4. On relief 8th Royal Scots Fusiliers and 12th Argyll & Sutherland Highrs will withdraw to billets at BRAY.

5. Completion of reliefs to be reported to Brigade Headquarters.

Acknowledge.

                               Major.

27.10.15.   Brigade Major 77th Infantry Brigade.

Copies to
8th Royal Scots Fusiliers.	1st Norfolk Regt.	5th Division.
11th Scottish Rifles.	1st Bedford Regt.	26th Division.
10th Black Watch.	13th Brigade.	
12th A. & S. Highrs.	15th Brigade.	

APP 20

5th Division.
G.B. 56/8

Moves on 29th instant will be as follows :-

1. Battalions of 15th Infantry Brigade marching to BRAY from SAILLY LORETTE to march so that the leading battalion passes Point 80 on BRAY - CORBIE road at 5.45 p.m. Route via Pt.105.

2. Two battalions of 77th Infantry Brigade marching to SAILLY LORETTE from BRAY, will pass Point 80 on BRAY - CORBIE Road at 5.15 p.m. and 5.45 p.m. respectively. Route via Pt. 105.

3. Brigade Headquarters of 15th and 77th Infantry Brigades will move to BRAY and SAILLY LORETTE respectively, under arrangements to be made mutually. 77th Infantry Brigade Signal section now working lines in 13th Inf. Bde. area, will be relieved by 13th Inf. Bde. Signal Section during the morning.

4. Battalions of 15th Infantry Brigade marching to BRAY will take over billets vacated by battalions of the 77th Infantry Brigade and vice versa, under arrangements to be made between the Brigades concerned.

5. 203rd Train Company will march independently during daylight from ETINEHEM to SAILLY-LE-SEC, but must be clear of SAILLY LORETTE by 2.30 p.m. O.C. 5th Div. Train is arranging accommodation in SAILLY-LE-SEC.

6. A.P.M. will arrange for road control at Point 80.

5th Division,
28.10.1915.

Lt.Colonel,
General Staff, 5th Division.

Copies to -
    5th Div. 'Q'.
    A.P.M.
    15th Inf. Bde.
    13th   "   "
    77th   "   "
    Div. Train.
    5th Signal Co.

MOVE 77th BRIGADE. B. M. 101

APP 20

Following movements will take place tomorrow 29th instant:

1. 12th Argyll & Sutherland Highrs and 8th Royal Scots Fusiliers from Bray into Billets at Sailly Morette.

2. Head of 12th Argyll & Sutherland Highrs will pass point 80 on BRAY - CORBIE road at 5.15 p.m. and 8th Royal Scots Fusiliers same point at 5.45 p.m. Route of both Battalions via Pt. 105.

3. Brigade Headquarters under the Staff Captain will march immediately in front of 8th Royal Scots Fusiliers.

4. Billeting parties from both Battalions will report to Staff Captain 15th Brigade at Sailly Lorette 2 p.m.

5. Arrival of Battalions in billets to be reported to Brigade Headquarters, Sailly Lorette.

Ackunsledge-

28.10.15.

Major.
Brigade Major 77th Infantry Brigade.

Copies to
8th Royal Scots Fusiliers.
11th Scottish Rifles.
10th Black Watch.
12th A. & S. Highrs.
203rd Coy. A.S.C.
15th Infy. Brigade.
5th Division.
26th Division.

SECRET.   Copy No. 7

                26th Division Order No. 9.   APP 21

                                        27th October, 1915.

   With reference to 5th Divisional Order No. 75 (a
copy of which has been forwarded to those concerned) the
moves of the 77th and 79th Infantry Brigades will take place
on the 29th and 30th insts., in accordance with the attached
March Table.

   ACKNOWLEDGE.

                                        R.W. Hare.
                                            Lieut. Colonel,
                                    General Staff, 26th Division.

Issued at   p.m. to:

G.O.C.   26th Divl. Train.
G.S.O.1.   8th Ox. and Bucks. L.I.(Pioneers).
A.A. and Q.M.G.   1st Lothian & Border Horse.
A.P.M.   26th Cyclist Company.
D.A.D.O.S.   26th Signal Company.
A.D.V.S.   A.D.M.S.
77th Infantry Brigade.   War Diary.   File.
78th Infantry Brigade.   18th Division (for information).
79th Infantry Brigade.   5th Division   do.
26th Divl. R.A.   10th Corps.   do.
26th Divl. R.E.

MARCH TABLE.

Moves to take place on 29th and 30th October, 1915.

Unit.	Starting Point.	Time.	Destination.	Route.	Remarks.
29th October.					
79th In.Bde. 12th Hants. (2 Coys.)	CARDONNETTE.		VAUX SUR SOMME.	ALLONVILLE-QUERRIEUX-PONT NOYELLES-CORBIE.	
30th October.					
77th In.Bde.	VAUX SUR SOMME.	9.0 a.m.	VILLERS BOCAGE. COISY. CARDONNETTE. RAINNEVILLE.	CORBIE--PONT NOYELLES- QUERRIEUX.	H.Q. and 1 Battalion and No. 2 Company Train to VILLERS BOCAGE. 1 Battn. to COISY, CARDONNETTE, RAINNEVILLE. To billet under Brigade arrangements.
79th In.Bde. (less 2 Bns.)	Cross roads ½m. N.W. of ALLON-VILLE.	9.0 a.m.	SAILLY LORETTE- CHIPILLY.	ALLONVILLE-QUERRIEUX-PONT NOYELLES-CORBIE	Billeting arrangements in accordance with 5th Divn. Order No. 75 dated 27th October.
12th Hants. (2 Coys.)	VAUX SUR SOMME.		ETINEHEM.		

SECRET.   77th Infantry Brigade.

MOVE.   B. M. 94

Reference AMIENS sheet 12.

1. In accordance with 26th Division order No. 9, the Brigade will move into billets 26th Divisional area on 30th instant, in accordance with attached March Table.

2. Cookers, water-carts, and all first line transport will follow in rear of Battalions.

   2nd Line transport will march in rear of Brigade under Brigade Transport Officer.

   2nd Line Transport of 12th Argyll & Sutherland Highrs and 8th Royal Scots Fusiliers will not leave SAILLY LORETTE till 10th Black Watch has passed through – road to be kept clear.

   From SAILLY LORETTE to VAUX order of march of transport in rear of Black Watch will be that of 12th Argyll & Sutherland Highrs, 8th Royal Scots Fusiliers, and 10th Black Watch.

   From VAUX onwards transport of 11th Scottish Rifles will march in front.

3. The Brigade will halt at 11 a.m. for two hours when clear of LA NEUVILLE (N.W. of CORBIE) for dinners.

   2nd Line Transport should water in neighbourhood of LA NEUVILLE. Great care is to be taken not to block the roads.

   Animals of 1st Line Transport may be sent to water at ~~once~~ O. C. units discretion, during two hours halt.

4. Regimental Billeting parties, on horses or cycles, will report at the head of the column 12 noon.

5. The Brigade will refill for the 31st instant on the march at cross roads RAINEVILLE QUERRIEUX ¾ mile N of B in BOIS de MAI.

The Transport of all Battalions will leave the column on arrival at above point, moving to Battalion billets independently after refilling.

6. Arrival in billets will be reported Brigade Head Quarters at VILLERS BOCAGE.

Acknowledge.

28-10-15

[signature] Major

Brigade Major 77th Infantry Brigade

Copies to
8th R. S. F.
11th S. R.
10th B.W.
203 Coy A.S.C. 12th A. & S. H.
Supply Officer O. C. Signal Sec.
Bde Transport Officer
5th Division
26th Division.

A21

MARCH TABLE.

Unit	Starting Point	Time	Destination	Route	Remarks
Hdqrs & Signal Sec 11th S.R.	Vaux (Church)	9 am	Villers Bocage	Corbie - Pont Noyelles - Querrieux	Leave Sailly Lorette 7.40 a.m.
12th A&SH	do.	9 am	do.	do.	Leave Sailly Lorette 7.45 am. Leave column at Raineville turn S W for Coisy
8th K.S.F.	do.	9.5 am	Coisy	do.	Leave Sailly Lorette 7.50 am. Leave column at Raineville
10th B.V.	do.	9.10 am	Raineville	do.	Leave Etinehem at 6 am Leave Chipilly 7 a.m.
Transport Brigaded	do.	9.15 am	Cardonnette	do.	
	do.	9.20 am	Battalion billets	via above and refilling pt	

Secret Draft

A 21

MOVE   77th Brigade   B. M. 94/1.

Reference B. M. 94 of 28th instant.

Owing to the road between Querrieux and cross roads N of B in Bois de Mal being bad the Brigade will march from Querrieux to Villers Bocage via Allonville and Coisy.

Units will leave Column as under for destinations.

10th Black Watch, cross roads ½ mile S of D in CARDONNETTE

8th R. S. Fusiliers cross road 1½ miles S.W. of RAINNVille.

12th A. & S. Highrs at COISY.

Except vehicles for refilling point 2nd Line Transport will continue to march in rear of Brigade, that of Black Watch Royal Scots Fusiliers and Argyll & Sutherland Highrs following their Battalions when the latter leave the column.

Vehicles for Refilling Point will march from Querrioux via St. Gratien.

Acknowledge.

                                       Major.

29.10.15.   Brigade Major 77th Infantry Brigade.

Copies to
8th Royal S. Fusiliers 2 copies.
11th S. Rifles.   do
10th B. Watch   do.
12th A. & S. Highrs   do.
203rd Coy. A.S.C.
Supply Officer.
Transport Officer Black Watch.
5th Division.
26th Division.

Secret

77th Brigade.

The Brigadier-General Commanding wishes to express to all ranks in the Brigade his appreciation of the soldierly conduct and bearing of the Brigade during the recent attachment to the 5th Division, both when Battalions were under instruction with older Brigades and also latterly when the Brigade was holding Sector C.

The two Battalions holding the left of the Sector had the experience of a mine explosion.

On both occasions the behaviour of the Officers and other ranks was very creditable, and the prompt and energetic way in which the damage done was repaired showed the possession of that discipline which is essential to the reputation of a Regiment.

The Grenadiers of both Battalions showed their appreciation of what their duties are, by their immediate and fearless action.

The two battalions holding the right of the Sector although they did not have the experience of mine explosions, carried out their duties which fell to their lot in an equally creditable manner.

The march of the Brigade yesterday was what a March should be.

The Brigade having begun to make a reputation it behoves it to live up to it and add to it and not live on it.

Major.

31.10.15.   Brigade Major 77th Infantry Brigade.

Return showing number of Casualties in
77th Infantry Brigade during attachment to 5th Division.

Unit	Officers		Other Ranks		Remarks
	Killed	Wounded	Killed	Wounded	
8th Royal S. Fus	-	1	1	1	
11th Sco Rifles	-	2	2	9	
10th Black Watch	-	x 2	4	9	x Accidental grenade exploding
12th A. & S. Highrs	-	1	3	8	
Total	-	4	9	27	

1.11.15

12/36th Division

121/6971

8th Royal Scots Fusiliers
Vol: I
Sept. 15 + Oct

J.H.

Army Form C. 2118.

WAR DIARY
~~INTELLIGENCE SUMMARY.~~
(Erase heading not required.)

8th Bn. ROY. SCOTS FUSILIERS
77th Brigade 26th Division
12th Army Corps, III Army.

Place	Date	Hour	Summary of Events and Information	Remarks and references to Appendices
FOLKESTONE	20/9/15		The personnel of the Battalion embarked for BOULOGNE. Strength 27 Officers 875 other ranks, one man who was absent on embarkation not included in this total.	J.A.W.B.
SOUTHAMPTON	20/9/15		The Transport and 3 Officers 109 Other ranks embarked at SOUTHAMPTON for HAVRE. Total attached 1 Medical Officer. 1 Staff Sergt A.O.C. 1 Private R.A.M.C. 6 Drivers A.S.C. Names of Officers. Headquarters Lieut-Col. H.V.BUNBURY. Major F.E.BUCHANAN. Captain and Adjutant J.A.McEWEN, Lieut. T.K.MURRAY, M.Gun Officer. Lieut. & Quartermaster S. LOVE. Lieut. J.V.GRANT. R.A.M.C. (attached). "A" Coy. Major R.M.CHRISTIE, Capt E.J.McPHAIL, Lieut W.R.HUTCHISON, 2nd Lieuts. R. LAMB. A.S. DIXON, S.C. HILLIARD. "B" Coy Captains W.E.PAUL, J.G.GRAHAM. Lieut. J.F.CAMPBELL. 2nd Lieuts. R.W. HUNTER G. McOWAN. C.N.CRAWSHAW, "C" Coy Captains M.R.DICKSON. R.W.GEDDES, Lieuts W.R.SCOTT, E.W.LANGLANDS. 2nd Lieuts. R. PATRICK. A. MITCHELL (Transport Officer) "D" Coy Captains C.P.REA, H.B.DUNCAN, Lieuts. R.A.MURRAY, W.GORDON-HALL. A.M. KENNEDY, 2nd Lieut R.S. POOLEY.	J.A.W.B.
BOULOGNE	21/9/15	1 A.M.	Disembarked and marched to OSTROHOVE Rest Camp.	
"	"	3 P.M.	marched to GARE AUTRALE railway station and entrained	J.A.W.B.
SALEUX	22/9/15	8 P.M.	Detrained at SALEUX and marched to FRICAMP arriving there at 3 A.M. 22/9/15 and billeted in village. The Transport and details which had travelled	

Army Form C. 2118.

WAR DIARY
~~INTELLIGENCE SUMMARY~~
(Erase heading not required.)

Instructions regarding War Diaries and Intelligence Summaries are contained in F. S. Regs., Part II. and the Staff Manual respectively. Title pages will be prepared in manuscript.

Place	Date	Hour	Summary of Events and Information	Remarks and references to Appendices
FRICAMPS	22/9/15		via SOUTHAMPTON and HAVRE, were at FRICAMPS when the personnel of the battalion arrived there	J. A. W2.
"	23/9/15	4 P.M.	Marched to PONT DE METZ arriving at 12.30 AM 24/9/15 and billetted. The Billets were very inferior and heavy rain fell during the night. One man who was absent on embarkation at FOLKESTONE was handed over by the 78th Brigade	J. A. W2.
PONT DE METZ	24/9/15	9 AM	Marched to VILLERS-BRETTONNEUX, via ST. ACHEUL and AMIENS. arrived at 3 p.m and billeted. in No 3 area.	J. A. W2.
VILLERS BRETONN- EUX	25/9/15		In Billets much rain; Resting & cleaning kit	J. A. W2.
"	26/9/15		In Billets Inspections & refitting. Test gas helmets. Sunday.	J. A. W2.
"	27/9/15		In Billets Rain. Sky overcast Route march.	J. A. W2.
"	28/9/15		In Billets Rain Training. Rapid loading, Rapid Fire, Bayonet, Physical Training	J. A. W2.
"	29/9/15		In Billets Rain Cold Wind. Training as above also The Charge, Field Kit	J. A. W2.
"	30/9/15		In Billets Cold. Training as above Inspection	J. A. W2.

121/7517

L.H.
5 sheets

26th Division

8th R.S. Fusiliers
Vol: 2
Oct 15

L.H.
5 sheets

WAR DIARY
or
INTELLIGENCE SUMMARY.

No. 2.   of   8th Bn. Royal Scots Fusiliers   Army Form C. 2118.

(Erase heading not required.)

Place	Date	Hour	Summary of Events and Information	Remarks and references to Appendices
Villers-Bretonneux	1/10/15		In Billets. Weather dry and chilly. Battalion went for a Route March 8-30 A.M. to 12.30 P.M.	J. A. W. B.
"	2/10/15		In Billets. Battalion packed up with all transport ready to move at 10 a.m. Move did not take place. Battn. paraded with 1st line transport at 2.15 p.m. for inspection by Genl. Munro Commdg. III Army. The day was exceptionally fine. Returned to billets from inspection at 5 p.m.	J. A. W. B.
"	3/10/15		In Billets. Church Parades in forenoon. Companies went for a short march in afternoon. Weather still good.	J. A. W. B.
"	4/10/15		In Billets. Battalion marched out in forenoon for training. Coy. parades in afternoon	J. A. W. B.
"	5/10/15	10 a.m.	The Battalion marched via ABANCOURT, MORCOURT, MERICOURT SUR SOMME to PROYART arriving at 3.30 P.M. Raining. Billeted in PROYART attached to the 81st Brigade for instruction in trenches.	J. A. W. B.
PROYART	6/10/15	8 a.m.	"A" and "B" Coys. march from PROYART to be attached to Gloster Regt. and 1st Bn Royal Scots in trenches near CAPPY, and CAPPY-LES-FONTAINE respectively for 48 hours. "C" "D" Coys. remain in billets at PROYART.	J. A. W. B.

WAR DIARY
INTELLIGENCE SUMMARY

8th Bn. Royal Scots Fusiliers

Army Form C. 2118.

No. 3

Place	Date	Hour	Summary of Events and Information	Remarks and references to Appendices
PROYART.	7/10/15		A. & B. Coys still in trenches. C. & D. Coys in billets in PROYART. No 9760 Pte Matthews "B" Coy was killed by splinter of shell while in fire trench.	J.A.W.E
	8/10/15		A. & B. Coys returned to billets in PROYART and C. & D. Coys went into trenches "C" Coy was attached to 2nd Bn Cameron Highlanders which relieved 1st Bn Royal Scots and "D" Coy was attached to 1st Bn Argyll & Sutherland Highlanders. No casualties.	J.A.W.E
	9/10/15		A. & B. Coys still in Billets at PROYART. C. & D. Coys still in trenches.	J.A.W.E
	10/10/15		The Battalion returned to VILLERS BRETONNEUX. and went into Billets	J.A.W.E
	11/10/15		In billets in VILLERS BRETONNEUX	J.A.W.E
	12/10/15		Lieut Col H.V. BUNBURY vacated command of the Battalion, which was assumed by Major F.E. BUCHANAN. The battalion marched to VAUX-SUR-SOMME.	J.A.W.E
	13/10/15		In Billets VAUX-SUR-SOMME	J.A.W.E
	14/10/15		In Billets VAUX-SUR-SOMME	J.A.W.E
	15/10/15		Marched to BRAY.	J.A.W.E
	16/10/15		In Billets BRAY.	J.A.W.E
	17/10/15		In Billets BRAY. The Battalion marched at 5.15 p.m. to trenches and relieved 1st Bn Dorset Regiment in trenches C.1 sector.	J.A.W.E
	18/10/15		In trenches. One man wounded to Lee Cspl Burrows "A" Coy with trench mortar. Considerable amount of sniping	J.A.W.E

No 4

WAR DIARY

INTELLIGENCE SUMMARY

8th Bn Royal Scots Fusiliers Army Form C. 2118.

Instructions regarding War Diaries and Intelligence Summaries are contained in F. S. Regs., Part II. and the Staff Manual respectively. Title pages will be prepared in manuscript.

(Erase heading not required.)

Place	Date	Hour	Summary of Events and Information	Remarks and references to Appendices
BRAY	19/10/15		In trenches. C.1 sector. Nothing unusual received	Jaw8
	20/10/15		In trenches. C.1 sector. Nothing unusual received	Jaw8
	21/10/15		In trenches. Relieved by 10th Black Watch 8.45 pm, and returned to billets BRAY	Jaw8
	22/10/15		In Billets BRAY	Jaw8
	23/10/15		In Billets BRAY	Jaw8
	24/10/15		In Billets BRAY. marched to C.1 Sector at 5.15 P.M. and took over trenches from 10th Bn Black Watch	J.a.w8
	25/10/15		In C.1 Sector trenches opposite village of MAMETZ, which was held by Germans	J.a.w8
	26/10/15		In C.1 Sector trenches Situation Normal Wet	J.a.w8
	27/10/15		In C.1 Sector trenches Situation normal	J.a.w8
	28/10/15		In C.1 Sector trenches Situation normal Battalion was relieved by 1st Battn. Bedfords Regiment and returned to billets in BRAY. RAINING, trenches very wet.	J.a.w8
	29/10/15		In Billets BRAY. at 5.15 pm. marched to SAILLY-LORETTE and went into billets	J.a.w8
	30/10/15		marched to RAINNEVILLE and went into billets	J.a.w8
	31/10/15		In Billets. RAINNEVILLE.	J.a.w8

12/7608

26th Division

10th Machine Vehicle (Royal Highlanders)
Vol I & 2

Sept & Oct. 15

Army Form C. 2118.

WAR DIARY
INTELLIGENCE SUMMARY.
(Erase heading not required.)

10th (Service) Battn. The BLACK WATCH.

WAR DIARY

of 10th Service Batt: The BLACK WATCH.

INTELLIGENCE SUMMARY.

Army Form C. 2118.
Vol. I
Page 1.

CONFIDENTIAL

Instructions regarding War Diaries and Intelligence Summaries are contained in F.S. Regs., Part II. and the Staff Manual respectively. Title pages will be prepared in manuscript.

Place	Date	Hour	Summary of Events and Information	Remarks and references to Appendices
SUTTON VENY WILTSHIRE	10.9.15		Mobilization completed.	
	17.9.15	8.15 p.m.	Forward party of MAJOR T. HARVEY, LT. J.B. CALDWELL, an 2/LT. W. J. DUFFY + 109 other ranks left for overseas, arriving SOUTHAMPTON 10.15 p.m.	
	18.9.15	4.15 p.m.	Forward party left SOUTHAMPTON arriving HAVRE 6.0 a.m. 19th inst. Four horses were cast + replaced by remount authority at SHARP SOUTHAMPTON. Weaker train (cal + light fd).	
HAVRE	19.9.15	6.0 p.m.	Forward party left HAVRE. French system of wire entrainment (bad: light fd).	
BOUGAINVILLE	20.9.15	6.0 a.m.	" arrived LONGUEAU, S.E of AMIENS. Marched at once to BOUGAINVILLE + billeted. march of 20 miles. Arrived BGN 4.30 p.m.	
SUTTON VENY	19.9.15	3.30 p.m.	Remainder of Batt: (2/LT LT Col W.S. DICK-CUNYNGHAM, CAPTS M.W. GLOAG, J.P. STURROCK, J.S. MACLEOD, J. M'LAUCHLAN, E.M. LITHGOW, W. STEWART, I.C. SANDERSON(Adjt), LT R.C.H. MILLAR, C.A. NICOL, J.M. SCOTT, R.M. DON, E.M. LITHGOW, W. STEWART, 2/LT M. M'DONALD, P. STORMONTH-DARLING, R.I.L. SCOTT, J.E. DENNISTON, W.M. MARTIN, E.G.M. PHILIPS, A.W.R. DON, H.A.F. M'LAREN, D. MATHIESON, I.B. GOW, G.P. KIRKPATRICK, A.O. DRYDALE and LT G.W. CHRISTIE RAMC (attached) left for FOLKESTONE, with 858 other ranks, arriving 8.45 p.m. at the docks. Whole party embarked but was disembarked owing to breakdown of floating wing. Marched to SHORNCLIFFE + bivouacked in camp. Owing to pressure of	
SHORNCLIFFE	20.9.15		Canadians, several cases of drunkenness ensuing. Left bivouac at 8.0 p.m., two trains being arrange, + marched to FOLKESTONE (Some Scottish + umble) (two boat-load) and arrived BOULOGNE midnight (two boat-load). Marched to OSTROHOVE camp + went into Scottish Rifles by late hour.	
BOULOGNE	21.9.15	8.0 a.m.	Full for the night. Few others report, having arrived with AMIENS, R.T.O. remarking it was the best entrainment he had seen. Arrived SALEUX 2.40 p.m. R.T.O. reports orders marched to GARE CENTRALE + entrained for SALEUX, near AMIENS, SALEUX was not good seem Arrived SALEUX 2.40 p.m. R.T.O. reports orders wait for orders. Batt: took shelter in shop of barn + had March to BOUGAINVILLE came awaited, but of TAUBES.	
		5.0 p.m.	Batt: marched 15 miles to BOUGAINVILLE. Men had not had sufficient rest of new pursuant Saw nothing. Very sharp at trotting fill late 15 miles, when very sharp falling at trotty. Men had not had sufficient rest of new took all were got in safely but arriving at	

2353 Wt. W25141454 700,000 5/15 D. D. & L. A.D.S.S./Forms/C. 2118.

WAR DIARY

of 10th Service Batt'n THE BLACK WATCH

INTELLIGENCE SUMMARY

Army Form C. 2118.

Vol. I
Page 2.

CONFIDENTIAL

(Erase heading not required.)

Place	Date	Hour	Summary of Events and Information	Remarks and references to Appendices
BOUGAINVILLE	22.9.15	11.0 pm	BOUGAINVILLE at 11.0 pm, where forward party met us, + billeted. Billets good. Weather warm + fine.	
	23.9.15	2.30 pm	Order to march to SALEUX + bivouac. Ready to move at 4 pm. Had to requisition 3 carts for kits with sick feet. Left at 4.50 pm, arriving SALEUX 9.45 pm. Weather bad, heavy rain with men. Went on to Gare SALOUEL + billeted for the night. MAJOR LIVINGSTONE from staff	
SALOUEL	24.9.15	9.0 am	Weather improved. Left for VILLERS-BRETONNEUX, 14 miles, the remainder as a brigade. BLACK WATCH in rear. Rte nr AMIENS. Men marched splendidly, 61 men were carried on carts from the start. Batt: on the march was very inspiring. On the march 4 when fell out + came along in motor lorries but the men were simply splendid + that it was a very fine Battalion (2) Sir splendid men who marched (2) Sir HENRY WILSON, CORPS COMMANDER, inspected by (1) Sir Mackenzie Kennedy 2/5th Division unordered splendid + that it was a very fine Battalion (2) Sir splendid men were in orders who sk(ipped) to congratulate the C.O. on the splendid way the men marched.	Ref:—
VILLERS-BRETONNEUX		3.0 pm	Arrived VILLERS-BRETONNEUX about 3.30 pm + billeted.	AMIENS Sheet 12
	25.9.15		Weather bad, rain all day. Remained in billets all day.	
	26.9.15		Got the last Demonstration, all ranks going through trenches of a new filled with gas. Rain.	
	27.9.15		Coy work + march past Brigadier General Sir Hugh. H. Stewart. Rain.	
	28.9.15	2.30 pm	Battn ordered to stand by ready to move at 10 a.m. went day. Order cancelled 9.30 pm	
	29.9.15	10.5 am	Battn ordered to stand by ready, to move at 1 p.m. Moved at 1 p.m. + arrived PROYART at 5.45 p.m. Service + 1st Reserve & Detachments M.G. with 2/Lt J. Duffy, R.J.L. SCOTT, W.M. MARTIN, G.P. KIRKPATRICK # SAA carts + HT carts + transport men to correspond (100 all ranks) was left at BRETONNEUX BILLETED at PROYART. 2/Lt I.B. Gow + 2nd Ambulance for the parachute, Rainy + cold.	
PROYART	30.9.15	6 a.m	A + D Coys. Capt T.S. LACLEOD + M.W. GLOAG, attached to 2/DCLI provided to trenches for 48 hours. B + C Coys attached to ROYAL IRISH FUSILIERS received instructions from them in trench work. 2/Lt I.B. GOW admitted to Fd Ambulance, owing to ? of trench. Weather better.	

2353 Wt. W2544/1454 700,000 5/15 D.D.&L. A.D.S.S. (Form) C. 2118.

WAR DIARY

of 1st & 10th Service Batt. "THE BLACK WATCH"

INTELLIGENCE SUMMARY.

CONFIDENTIAL   (Erase heading not required.)

Army Form C. 2118.

Vol I
Page 3.

Place	Date	Hour	Summary of Events and Information	Remarks and references to Appendices
PROYART	2.10.16	6 a.m.	B & D Coys proceeded to trenches 1½ miles W. of FONTAINE-LES-CAPPY. 2/D.C.L.I. had been relieved previous day by ROYAL IRISH FUSILIERS, to whom A & D Coys had now attached. Relief of 2/R.I.F. & 2/D.C.L.I. Coys took place at 8.30 a.m. by platoons at intervals of 1/4 hour. Sitting of trenches an undulating & barely wooded ground permitted relief in daylight. B & C Coys left trenches at 5 a.m. 4/10/15. No casualties occurred in Battn. also several cases reported of snipers fire. Coys went forward to 5/5,5b in two bays, 2/D.C.L.I. and R.I.F. occupied all shelters. Trenches were slightly enfiladed by German lines, owing to salient. Idea that siting a narrow slope oriented [?]. But aeroplanes cannot spot any trench in the open & commanding view of our trench [?]. Trenches had been built by the French & were T shaped. They consist of its up being connected. Much had then been to connect up + complete connection and arrange establish. Two salients ran out from a wood known as BOIS COMMUN having + counter-mining was apparently carried in their ahead. Two craters 20' and 60' deep. 2'H.F. in trenches. The approach lines led at a distance of some 20 yards. The mining operations at this point [?] [?] appeared to be leading to any definite result. 2 hrs has had day but from the base of little dolmite [?] were very strong stands into sandbag behind communication trenches [?] were altogether too few, but they had gradually being rearranged. The hat front occupied by Batt. was 2000 yards + consequently very lightly held. M.G. emplacements were well-placed for enfilade fire. Parapet was not broad enough. Loud sort of front + knee deep Rural Squads + Hammer Sprayers will not all in working order.	Ref. AMIENS Sheet 12.
FONTAINE LES CAPPY				

WAR DIARY
of 10th (SERVICE) BATT" THE BLACK WATCH
INTELLIGENCE SUMMARY

Army Form C. 2118
Vol I, Page 4.

Place	Date	Hour	Summary of Events and Information	Remarks and references to Appendices
FONTAINE LES CAPPY	3.10.15		No rifle racks were provided nor was there any arrangement for rifle battening. There was not enfilachment for Batt: left by the French. Latrines accommodation was bad, but was hung inborns in the intervention of the trench system. The French apparently did not accustomed to dig holes in the ground & cover them up. When full. Shelters for the men in communicating trenches, close to the fire trench, not good, but were made to accommodate too large a number in each shelter. But it is better objection was that unless be that they had an entrance at sixteen and on to a communicating trench. The consumption of trench grenades was so heavy. A sector is long + should be avoided. It only contains the men for twenty four hours & rations were brought by hand from a point close to Batt Hqrs in the village. advisable, if possible, to have rations cooked at a spot some distance behind from Batt Hqrs to avoid the long. Telephonic communication was kept good — probably faulty insulation & with heavy 2 cops are linked from an exchange station, so that Batt Hqrs can be heard by Hqrs at the reserve trenches & by HQ (i.e.) to a variety of points in front & in the trenches, and, if you use this instruments a single switch arrangement from our (i.e.) communicates to Brigade so as to include a third rifle trans (or any other attacks. saying it would be useful in case of attack to be all concerned. The men (when) in the trenches was and for thirty six hour ought to all concerned, at night, in a big Br. connecting very well + natural well as working parties controls if we are working 4½ to the lt. trenches. Men working parties for the undrainable. The Battalion received orders from the General day last (an hour) 27/16 Division. for the undrainable. It was likely to except can a turn, a hostile shell have exploded 10 men.	Ref. AMIENS Sheet - 12

W.G. Sandeman
Capt HQs

WAR DIARY of 1st Service Batt'n, The Black Watch

Army Form C. 2118.
Vol. I Page 5.

INTELLIGENCE SUMMARY

CONFIDENTIAL. (Erase heading not required.)

Place	Date	Hour	Summary of Events and Information	Remarks and references to Appendices
CAPPY	3.10.15		The Service + 1st Reserve Machine Gun Detachments of the Batt'n, which had been left behind at VILLERS-BRETONNEUX proceeded on 3rd October to CAPPY + were attached to Princess Patricia's LIGHT INFANTRY for two days' trench work. Reserve Section were in for one night + were relieved the next day. The P.P.L.I. had no alternative emplacements (but on detachment arriving they were to put their own gun into them, also they had no retaining rides. Our 4 teams emplaced over the corner a march where night rites has to fire. Any trenches + which was protected only by battle's at night. Owing to the fact that the British line ran in the John of a night angle the village of FRISE and only about 900 yards from a trench tangle. The intersection of French had some catacombs by the French which was run through the line + had all been supped by an M.G.O. was extended by the P.P.L.I. On arrival on night, on by the delivery officer - took him round being to find a guide from each emplacement for the reliming section + himself to meet the relief officer + "the Trenches + beneath collecting his relieved men at the "sump" as the dirty was always on duty in each marching them back to billets. I sensed within kicking distance emplacement + an Stm men always kept very slight women't, men Two casualties occurred from a shell that day. The two detachments returned to returning to duty next day. The 6th Oct. VILLERS-BRETONNEUX on the 6th Oct.	Ref. to AMIENS Sheet 12
VILLERS-BRETONNEUX	6.10.15			
	8.10.15		The Batt'n was inspected at having by Sir HENRY WILSON commanding 12th Corps who said his had good account of the Regiment from the this lay his 12th Division to which it had been (commanded) attached for French instruction.	J. Harden Col.

WAR DIARY

of 1/10th Batt: The Black Watch.

INTELLIGENCE SUMMARY.

Army Form C. 2118.
Vol I
Page 6.

Place	Date	Hour	Summary of Events and Information	Remarks and references to Appendices
VILLERS BRETONNEUX	11.10.15		Batt: received orders to move next day to CHIPILLY	Ref: AMIENS Sheet 12.
CHIPILLY	12.10.15	12.30pm	Moved at 12.30pm, having (about) 2/Lt C.S.L. Phillips + 16 other ranks at Gara Dr. Echon + in Station 16 other ranks left for medical reasons. Arrived CHIPILLY 3.35pm + billeted.	
BRAY-SUR-SOMME	13.10.15	5.35pm	Moved to BRAY-SUR-SOMME arriving there at 8.0pm + billeted.	
	14.10.15		C.O., 2nd in Command, Adjt, 4 Coy commanders + M.G.O reconnoitred trenches held by KING'S OWN YORKSHIRE LIGHT INFANTRY. Front about 1200x. Batt: moved out to relieve KOYLI at 5.30pm by Coys at intervals of 10 minutes. Platoon guides met Bn. Coys at CARNOY and drew Batt: Hqrs in sheets. Relief completed about 10.10pm. Transport was kept on in a special with rations + water. Takes a great difficulty to get near to coffee, etc. Leaving 4th Coy) and from RE's to half at 4.15 + tower transport + able 6.30pm in + Capt. Jacob not absent. Rations + water were brought up later in system or astyrka has been there by fatigue parties to my retain at men to Coy in front trouble + a fatigue team to carry all water parties were absent from Coys, when tanks at cookers had + also water. Water parties were meal day well. Sufficient for meal day well. A, C and D Coys (left trenches), Sherwood and Sloss) held the front trenches with 3 platoons per Coy, + one in out support, B Coy forming Batt: reserve. Strength handed in the night 14/15. 10-15. Normal being taken in. 24 nco men at left trenches on(?) left hand by J. White (acting M.O.T) 1st/4th(?) Gordons from(?) so Jaundice. Cept. 2nd I/cm, C. Wade (sugar) in Watkins + Wak. trans: known Bray Braks, Capt. J.S. Walker on 2/14 G.E. Dannister	
CARNOY	15.10.15	11-12 on		

J.C. Sanderson
Capt. Adjt.

WAR DIARY INTELLIGENCE SUMMARY

Army Form C. 2118.

WAR DIARY of 10th SERVICE BATT: The BLACK WATCH. Vol. I Page 7.

CONFIDENTIAL.

Place	Date	Hour	Summary of Events and Information	Remarks and references to Appendices
CARNOY	15/10/15	10pm	Cpl. of A Coy was wounded by & Pte. accidentally explosion of a grenade. 4 men of the Bomb. Platoon were killed.	REF to APPENDIX I
	16/10/15	7a.m.	Enemy fired two rifle grenades into D Coys trench (H5) one sniping killing two men & wounding two others. Position from which they were fired could not be located definitely. but battery retaliated by turning 12 trench mortar shrapnel rounds in shelling damage to personnel. One may was wounded in head whilst throwing trench mortar bombs. Our battries shelled M.G. Emplacement. Enemy trench-mortars always fire at transport at night. Personal Thresher by Coy commander which shots are always sent to artillery having no H.E. at shot. will aimed. Enemy fired little transport over our lines about 2.30 pm & about 30 F.O.O. support trench about 20 shrapnel over our left trenches close to Battn HQrs. No damage done to Personnel to become any loss that at night 10/17. probably of the personnel having targets any use. Wind was not out by night, nothack. Wind being south.	
	17/10/15		Enemy gun fired rifle grenades at trenches 51 and 53. Two men were wounded in Trench 51 one of whom died later. Trench 51 is always a target for grenade & should be held lightly. Trench mortars were fired just R of Trench 51 by enemy. Position of battery which banked & latter was observed by artillery. H.E. emplacement. Personally was boarding on road & was shelled. also shelled. RIFLES, Robert was wounded. Battn was relieved in the evening by 11 Scottish light M.E. & remained 7.15pm & was completed by 5.45pm. Wind light. held in front line a Special Reconnde Trenches approved of H.E. strongly held & to kill or wound) was than we were. how well placed ground was certain to the front line, & were communicating trenches Dug-outs were necessary on the front line. Work as being carried on continually on the from it to support line. Support lines but could probably have been	

J. Sanderson
Capt Adjt

Army Form C. 2118.

Vol I
Page 2

WAR DIARY
of 10th Service Battn. The
INTELLIGENCE SUMMARY. Black Watch
CONFIDENTIAL (Erase heading not required.)

Place	Date	Hour	Summary of Events and Information	Remarks and references to Appendices
CARNOY	18.10.15		applied with were advantage at the moment in hitting back shelters for men in front trench. Men went out a lineal to strip & shelter during the night, & as to trench, men the guy the sentries (?) not have bayonets fixed, but all other men had bayonets & the sniper placed in each (?) out at night, except in moonlight, ought also had his bayonet fixed. Beats: Here & the Dump, which are high, the men trench must have supplied every covering, and snipers to shoot bullets & to enfilade artillery fire. Snipers did not take advantage of this, but could have done so. It would have been better to have lain & high sands by a Sabre & hastily built to counter-attack and not possibility.	
BRAY-SUR-SOMME	19.10.15		Battn returned to WURH in BRAY. 200 men were employed highly + 200 men daily in fatigue work, which a support line B2 So Krustin.	
	20.10.15		Battn asked at BRAY, the out country chiefly in providing fatigue parties of from 50 to 100 men (totalling 250) diggers & carrying trenches in support & reserve lines.	
	21.10.15		Ditto at (?) Bray. Orders issued for relieving 8th ROYAL SCOTS FUSILIERS the evening of (?) 22nd with C.O., 2nd in command, Adjt., Q Commdrs, M.G.O. & S.t. being men and the C1 intacted in the meantime.	

J. NawSm(?)
Capt (?)

2353. Wt. W25414/1454 700,000 5/15 D.D.&L. A.D.S.S./Forms/C. 2118.

Army Form C. 2118.

Vol I
Page 9

WAR DIARY
or
INTELLIGENCE SUMMARY.
(Erase heading not required.)

Instructions regarding War Diaries and Intelligence Summaries are contained in F.S. Regs., Part II. and the Staff Manual respectively. Title pages will be prepared in manuscript.

Place	Date	Hour	Summary of Events and Information	Remarks and references to Appendices
CARNOY	21.10.15	5:15pm	Batt moved off by Coys between 5:15pm + 5:45pm. C + D Coys proceeding by road to F.28.6 ⅔ where nearest working road, when they were met by guides. A + B Coys moving by road to BRONFAY FARM, where guides took them over communication trenches. B + C Coys went in front trench, A + D Coys in support trenches. Relief was completed by 9:45pm. 4 Dorset Officers each attached, one to each Coy, from 15th Bn.	REF C5 ALBERT (on this) Sheet 57 D SE 57 C SE 62 D NE 62 C NW
			fairly quick.	
D, Black	22.10.15		4 hounitzes was fired over by trench + communication trench. Little damage done. 4 howitzers fired again about 11pm + there from 2&7pm to enemy's trench. Position minewerfer was located. One minewerfer was in our left flank our line in while working a repair line in near fire start. One man was killed by infantry fire. C & D sections also 66 + 67. Rebel reports was too weak + we were too far apart approx 65.	REF C5 APPENDIX II
	23.10.15		Four minewerfer were again sent over by trench about 10 approxpat in night. By it was known + two was extremely shaken + smashed by falling [?] sandbags. Smoke of fire burnt was blown over our trenches by night of MAMETZ village seemed to come from about the line which apparently came in short of Artillery bombard [?] that shot through trenches with good effect. a minewerfer crossed for the day. Our enemy artillery came on about 10 A.M. but not enough + shared much [?] M.G. fire on our infantry sniping unknown.	
			One was wounded by fire in while sniping. Enemy HAIE MORE heavy infantry fire later day + night, coming approach from our right both head falls in heavy post in 66 trench. Sniping was very active + our[?] shots continually came on our [?] the night and) from the war, it would appear that the position of during the enemy gun fell the emplacements of there is well known to the enemy. J Sheraton Capt Adjt

WAR DIARY
of 1st Bn. The BLACK WATCH
INTELLIGENCE SUMMARY

Army Form C. 2118.
Vol I
Page 10.

Place	Date	Hour	Summary of Events and Information	Remarks and references to Appendices
CARNOY CITADEL	24/10/15		The day was abnormally almost uncannily quiet, very little sniping going on. One man was killed while lighting a front Relief by a bullet which came stray through a sand bag. The back of his head was blown away, as if an explosive bullet had been used, but was found not to be so, so to which he was brought to. R.S. Farrelius taken completely. Relief was carried out at 6.30 p.m. Sand bagging. Relief completed at 8.20 p.m. by battalion marching billet k on plank. Relief completed at BRAY-SUR-SOMME. (Bill at BRAY-SUR-SOMME.) General. The trenches much very poor & there was no evidence of attention having been paid to them. Fire steps were bad, as were parapets & parados, in some cases too low. Strong left and in many places sandy. The parapet was not bullet proof. A great deal of work should probably be put in by the battn in improving the trenches generally. Dirt sandbag & brush revetment. Putting in flying traverse and new terches which were surprised D. Gap support line was also considerable rough latrines was bad, and & seek a sump pits had both been unpleasant by them attempt, and such as it sent were to drain to can't & was too generous to H.W. harbour and replacements were poor — they were too cramped and had to limited a field of fire and no better emplacement (?a) as a rest Our trying part of an Officer + 30 men was left in the trenches at 9pm. 24.10.15 as the fatigue party had A.A. been provided at 1.30 a.m. at a place known as the 'Citadel' about 1 mile behind the Battn H.Qrs & it was not until 5 am. that the fatigue fell back to billets first. It would seem rather an	REF to ALBERT complete sheet.
BRAY-SUR-SOMME	25/10/15			Sgd R. Sanderson

WAR DIARY
10th Batt: The BLACK WATCH
INTELLIGENCE SUMMARY
(Erase heading not required)
CONFIDENTIAL

Army Form C. 2118.
Vol I
Page 11.

Place	Date	Hour	Summary of Events and Information	Remarks and references to Appendices
26 Locks BRAY-SUR- SOMME	25/10/15 26/10/15		Nineteen prisoners to take a fatigue party at 1.30am from a Fatt: which had just left the trenches at 8pm. Batt: rested in billets promptly. 350 men for fatigue on subsidiary line. The same number (men were employed) on fatigue. One man was killed by rifle fire, while supplying on wiring fatigue in Cr. Sollecter.	REP:ce ALBERT (enclosed sketch)
ETINEHEM & CHIPILLY	27.10.15 28.10.15 29.10.15		Batt: moved at 5.0pm from BRAY and marched via ETINEHEM to CHIPILLY. 2 Coys were billeted at ETINEHEM, remainder and HQrs at CHIPILLY. Two companies at ETINEHEM were employed on fatigue in subsidiary line till 12 noon daily, supplying 300 men, as the further fatigue tho' the farm Jan 29.15 with at 12.30 from C Coy, and rest of four CHIPILLY to perform work. All 3 Coys A, B, and C returned to CHIPILLY, the ensuing by 2.45 Piset. after completion of fatigue. From two evening Batt: could ever only 2 6rs by 77th Bde Bn. again.	
CHIPILLY.			(from above) for march to CARDONETTE next day. Batt: paraded at 7.0am & marched for CARDONETTE. A halt and water was at LA NEUVILLE at 11.0AM. Batt: arrived at CARDONETTE and billeted 4.27pm when washed to B. writes with to sport to the many fatigues. They had been away from me & short one hoy only (returned at 11.50pm on transport. only six men fell out & had to be carried) owing to entirely in the field & included sick Batt: rested in billets. Strength of Batt: over to date 2/2/. W.F. BASSETT Com	REF: AMIENS Sheet 12
CARDON- ETTE.	30.9.15			
	31.10.15 (Sunday)		actually evacuated is over 300 to 94), not 27 Officers from 3rd Batlyn (Gazetted 10/5) joined the day.	W.F. BASSETT Capt AAT

Army Form C. 2118.

WAR DIARY
or
INTELLIGENCE SUMMARY.
(Erase heading not required.)

Instructions regarding War Diaries and Intelligence Summaries are contained in F. S. Regs., Part II. and the Staff Manual respectively. Title pages will be prepared in manuscript.

Place	Date	Hour	Summary of Events and Information	Remarks and references to Appendices
				APPENDIX II PLAN of TRENCHES C, Subsector CARNOY.

Scale 1/10,000

GERMAN. BLUE.
BRITISH. RED.

MAMETZ
To CONTALMAISON
HAIE NOIRE
MONTAUBAN
BRAY
to FRICOURT

CAMERONIANS
11th (Scottish Rifles)
Vol I

Sep. 15 1915

CONFIDENTIAL

WAR DIARY

of

11th   Scottish Rifles.

From September 1st 1915. to September 30th 1915.

(VOLUME 1.)

WAR DIARY or INTELLIGENCE SUMMARY

Army Form C. 2118

11th Scottish Rifles

Place	Date	Hour	Summary of Events and Information	Remarks and references to Appendices
SUTTON VENY WILTS	Sept 1 /15		The Regiment carried out its short course of musketry, and officers	
	Sep 18th		& men proceeded on 7 days leave previous to embarking for active service	HQ
	Sep 19th		We left in two special trains from WARMINSTER Station for FOLKESTONE. On arrival at SHORNCLIFFE CAMP Station, had to detrain, as transport Submarines had recently sunk a ship outside FOLKESTONE HARB. and all crossings to BOULOGNE had been cancelled. Marched up to the CAMP at 11pm. and bivouaced for the night in the open. Bitterly cold, most blowing. Strength on marching out 30 officers 942 other ranks, 12 chargers 20 horses & mules 21 pairs wheeled waggons 4 G.S. wheeled waggons.	HQ
		8pm	out of WARMINSTER	
			We moved from bivouac to lines of 17th Battn Canadian Regt, and were well looked after. Weather fine.	
SHORNCLIFFE CAMP and FOLKESTONE	Sep 20th	6pm	As the Battalion received orders not to move – They must not on a short route march. On returning at 7pm – orders had been received to entrain that night. – The left CAMP at 8.45pm, and reached FOLKESTONE PIER. 10pm. to embark in mail boat for BOULOGNE. Sailed at 10.45pm – The Qr.M. General (26th) with Staff were on board. Reached BOULOGNE at 12.30 am. – NOTE :– (The Vaughan's left SUTTON VENY on 18th and embarked at SOUTHAMPTON for HAVRE)	HQ

WAR DIARY
or
INTELLIGENCE SUMMARY

Army Form C. 2118

Place	Date	Hour	Summary of Events and Information	Remarks and references to Appendices
SILLEUX	Sep 21		Marched to REST CAMP from PIER. Arrived at 3am. Roused at 6am. Told by Staff Officer that we would not move today - Orders came at noon for the Regiment to entrain for SAILEUX at 1.45pm. This gave the Regiment 30 minutes to pack up, and leave the Rest Camp at 12.30pm. Detrained at SILLEUX 5pm. The railway carriages were awful, and most uncomfortable. Our Staff Captain (77th Bde) informed us that they did not know of our arrival, and no Transport could be obtained to march to our billets at BOUGANVILLE. We hired 2 carts and started from SAILEUX at 9pm - Fine moonlight night. After a 15 mile march we reached BOUGANVILLE at 3am - where our Transport from HAVRE had just arrived - The billets had been arranged, as they did not know we were coming - The Regt bivouced in a field beside the Transport.	COY
BOUGANVILLE	" 22		Got Officers and men into billets - fine weather at BOUGANVILLE - Water supply very bad.	HQD COY
	" 23		Left BOUGANVILLE at 4pm, and marched to PONT de METZ - name HQD COY HOD	
	" 24		harm all the way - Halted at 5pm and gave the men tea on roadside	

Army Form C. 2118

(3)

WAR DIARY
or
INTELLIGENCE SUMMARY
(Erase heading not required.)

Instructions regarding War Diaries and Intelligence Summaries are contained in F.S. Regs., Part II. and the Staff Manual respectively. Title Pages will be prepared in manuscript.

Place	Date	Hour	Summary of Events and Information	Remarks and references to Appendices
	Sep 24th		Reached Brest at 8pm, and had great difficulty in moving up internally, as they did not know of our arrival. Got settled midnight.	HQ
VILLERS BRETTONEAUX	Sep 25		Marched to VILLERS BRETTONEAUX at 7am — after leaving AMIENS was inspected on the march by Divisional Comdr. and Army Commander. HQ Arrived in billets 3pm. A long trying march the last two days with little sleep for the men. 1st day.	HQ
	Sep 26		At VILLERS BRETTONEAUX refitting	HQ
	" 27		do	HQ
	" 28		do	HQ
	" 29		Left for a tour of instruction in the Trenches — Marched at 1pm for CAPPY via MERICOURT. Arrived in billets 8pm and reported to Brigadier SMITH of 80th Brigade.	HQ
CAPPY	" 30th		Took Company Commanders into trenches of 4th K.R.R. at 2pm — (left half Battalion under Major DAVIDSON was attached to 2nd R.B. and SHROPSHIRE REGT.) went over the trenches with Right Half.	HQ
MOULIN		6pm.	Battn Commander at THE MOULIN and returned to CAPPY at 10.30pm. Marched from billets at 9.15pm, reached THE MOULIN at 11.30pm and got men into trenches at	

H.A. Thompson Lt Col

CONFIDENTIAL.

WAR DIARY

of

11TH SCOTTISH RIFLES.

From October 1st 1915 to October 31st, 1915.

VOLUME I.

WAR DIARY or INTELLIGENCE SUMMARY

Army Form C. 2118

11th Scottish Rifles

Place	Date	Hour	Summary of Events and Information	Remarks and references to Appendices
	Oct 1st	1 am	Went round Trenches at 1am with C.O. of 4th K.R.R. — all quiet — my men were mixed up with the Regular Batt'n for instruction. They were throwing spent cartridge case of ENGLAND creeping trenches for days at a time, so found the work easy to pick up. Every Batt'n seems to have its own system of working. These trenches had been recently taken over from the FRENCH and were in very rough order. Between 10·30 and 11 am the MOULIN was shelled and officers and men took to the Dug outs: at noon made a tour of inspection, as far as THE BOIS VERT along the trenches — met the 26th Div't and 77th Bde Commanders. At 2 pm enemy started shelling and throwing rifle grenades — No 15085 Pte MOORE was wounded. No 15100 Pte WOOD was wounded. Killed by a rifle grenade and No 14461 Pte MORAN was shot through the arm with a rifle bullet. Enemy kept up a hot shell fire during the afternoon of Shrapnell and trench mortars. The KRR had 3 killed and 4 wounded. The close connection with the R.A. was most useful in bringing a replied reply, which silenced the enemy for the time being. Visited the trenches at midnight. Weather fine.	11/20

MOULIN SUR SOMME

WAR DIARY or INTELLIGENCE SUMMARY

Army Form C. 2118 (2)

Place	Date	Hour	Summary of Events and Information	Remarks and references to Appendices
CAPPY	Oct 2		Buried 150/5 Ptr men at 7am in a little graveyard close to the SOMME. There was no R.C. Chaplain available at the time so in CO conducted the service. Lieut MORTIMORE and STRATHIE were present. Before the service was finished the enemy opened fire. Four previously, but the burial was completed in spite of this. Our enemy's aircraft made four previously, but the burial was completed in spite of this. Our men not left till 11-30. Fine warm day - marched out of the trenches at 7am, and not left till 11-30. Both new MAJOR DAVIDSON at CAPPY. They kept us cemetery Bivouced outside MERICOURT for the night - undisturbed in the early morning at 6am	Cap Cap
	Oct 3		Left MERICOURT and marched to VILLERS BRETTONEAUX, arriving at 1pm. Cool march - Brig Gen Sir Hugh Stewart met us, and marched in with the Regiment	Cap
VILLERS BRETTONEAUX	"	4th	At VILLERS BRETTONEAUX. Training and refitting	Cap
	"	5th		Cap
	"	6th		Cap
	"	7th		Cap
	"	8th		Cap
	"	9th	General Sir J. WILSON - 12th Army Corps, inspected the Regt at 10am Hd at drill. He saw the attack delivered from the trenches in two lines.	Cap
	"	10th	Church parade at 10 am - Muster parade 2-30pm.	Cap

WAR DIARY
or
INTELLIGENCE SUMMARY

(Erase heading not required.)

Army Form C. 2118

Place	Date	Hour	Summary of Events and Information	Remarks and references to Appendices
	Oct 11th		The Regt formed the "fighting piquets" of the Brigade. One Coy ready to turn out in marching order in 10 minutes - The other in 30 minutes - Gen Sir H. STEWART turned them out - They fell in, in 5 minutes and 15 minutes respectively.	Coy
SALLY LORETTE	12th		Left VILLERS BRETTONNEAUX at 1-30pm and marched to billets at SALLY LORETTE arriving at 3.45pm. Very hot short march. 5th Div inspected us as we marched in. MAJOR GEN P. KAVANAGH.	Coy Coy Coy Coy
	13th 14th 15th 16th		Bathing and washing parades in the SOMME. Training - and refitting. Left SALLY LORETTE at 4-30pm and reached BRAY at 6pm - The adjutant of the K.O.Y.L.I. was attached to the Regt. for instructional purposes in the trenches - The C.O. and Company Commanders rode forward and spent 3 hours in trenches (B2) to know their way up to the trenches and then up to a farm and then left our horses - about. Rode half way to a communicator trench.	Coy Coy Coy
BRAY	17th		On arrival in hut, in a communicator trench. The Regt found 20 men daily for fatigue duties; and R.E. Mining parties. This morning all the men had a bath in the 15 th/Div Baths, and clean clean clothes	Coy

Army Form C. 2118

WAR DIARY
or
INTELLIGENCE SUMMARY
(Erase heading not required.)

Place	Date	Hour	Summary of Events and Information	Remarks and references to Appendices
B₂ Trenches FARNOY	Oct 17		we came to Inur — In an experience of 30 years with the regular army — I have never seen a unit practice their drill for the comfort and health of the private soldier — Officers could have hot baths too. Left for B₂ Trenches at 5.15 p.m. in relief of 10th BLACK WATCH at FARNOY. Companies marched along the road at 10 minute intervals, as shelling had taken place lately. Line been moonlight night. Relief completed at 8 p.m.	
	18th		Went round trenches with Adjt NOYES at 4 a.m. — all quiet. Major DAVIDSON took half the distance — The Fire Trenches were fully 500 yds from the Support Time Companies were trying one gun or two in support. Very difficult getting water up to the men as the enemy was all over in the Bourne — most of the ford was stone and where it reached the river. Point Two to carry water, were very valuable articles — Men collected over 100 before going into trenches — Work at night consists of pulling up new wire entanglement, and sapping out to a new CRATER each the enemy had made. A French Bomb Battery did great work each evening about 5 p.m. — Two Officers patrols went out at midnight and brought back useful information — They consist of 1 officer and 1 private who lay out in front of enemy wire and listened —	1007

Army Form C. 2118

WAR DIARY
or
INTELLIGENCE SUMMARY
(Erase heading not required.)

Place	Date	Hour	Summary of Events and Information	Remarks and references to Appendices
Bry Junction DRANOY	Oct 19.		Working parties revetting parapets with sand bags, and building 2 new field defences. About 4pm No 14572 Pte J. McEWAN was shot through the head by a sniper. He was working at the top, already mentioned and unfortunately looked up above the trench was shot. The Royal WEST KENT Regt on our left had an afternoon with the enemy re hung up grenade bombs etc. They were supported by the artillery and did considerable damage to the enemy's trenches in front of them.	HQs
	Oct 20.		No 15700 Pte H. BROWN shot by a sniper about 3pm. Enemy's working party with machine digger reported by O.C. No 3 Co (Capt. DARBY) at 11am R.F.A. opened fire at once — The mind shell landed on the digger. Enemy's machine gun opened fire on our transport at 6.45pm. No casualties. K.O.S.B's No 16585 Pte W. BURT, wounded by a bomb. Relieved the Regt at 6.15pm. We marched back to Billets at BRAY	HQs
BRAY	"21 "22		at BRAY. Training and refitting.	HQs HQs
C2 CARNOY	"23		Left BRAY at 5.15pm, to relieve 12th Argyll and Sutherland High'rs in trenches at C2 (CARNOY). Bright moonlight night — Baggage came into trenches by light railway. Relief took place 8.15pm.	HQs ? Billet Etain.

Army Form C. 2118

6

WAR DIARY
or
INTELLIGENCE SUMMARY
(Erase heading not required.)

Instructions regarding War Diaries and Intelligence Summaries are contained in F. S. Regs., Part II. and the Staff Manual respectively. Title Pages will be prepared in manuscript.

Place	Date	Hour	Summary of Events and Information	Remarks and references to Appendices
{ C? Trenches FARGNY }	Oct 24		Very quiet morning — The R.E. Officer in charge of mines warned us to be prepared for the explosion of one of the enemies. Very quiet afternoon and evening	1943
	Oct 25		About 1:45 am. We were trenches short like an earthquake and at the same time the enemy opened a hot shell and rifle fire. The O. C. No 2 Company reported that a mine had been exploded in front of our trenches and a certain amount of damage had been done. The debris was cleared away by dawn and the parapet of fire trench repaired. Lieut GUNN was wounded in the wrist whilst clearing away the debris. The Company (No 2) were under fire all the time this work was being carried out. The Bombing Officer of THE CHESHIRE REGT. and mine exploded with Sergt GEDDES and Corporal FISHER & Lieut H. DANGERFIELD, immediately jumped over the parapet and also 9 regimental Bombers. We had to give it up, as the two held the new CRATER, until dawn. A sap head was sent our British CRATERS enfiladed the new one. Lieut H. DANGERFIELD was slightly down in at the time of the explosion and 5 men of the Regiment wounded when occupying the new CRATER, but would not report sick wounded and gassed.	1 2

WAR DIARY
INTELLIGENCE SUMMARY
(Erase heading not required.)

Army Form C. 2118

Instructions regarding War Diaries and Intelligence Summaries are contained in F.S. Regs., Part II. and the Staff Manual respectively. Title Pages will be prepared in manuscript.

Place: CARNOY (C2 Trenches)

Date	Hour	Summary of Events and Information	Remarks and references to Appendices
Oct 25		A howitzer battery came into action at Sker and did good work in shelling the survivors of the craters to destroy any new trenches they may have been digging. Cold and wet. The names of the wounded are WOUNDED. No 15553 Pte MOTT. No 15446 Pte HOLDEN " 15793 " PEDAN No 15133 Pte GALLACHER " 16018 " BORTHWICK.	(M) (M)
" 26		Fine bright morning. Owing to No 2 Co having had a very hard day of it yesterday- I brought up No 4 Coy (Capt YALDEN THOMSON) from the Piave, and let No 2 Coy rest. The parapets where numbers had exploded were put in a thoroughly safe condition and a sap started out to the new CRATER. At 1 p.m. a rifle grenade caused the following casualties. WOUNDED 2/Lieut KIRKPATRICK. J.C. No14430 Sgt MORLEY (since dead) No 14598 Pte CORRIGAN No 18542 Pte CLARKE These men were returning in a fire trench at the turn. 2/ KIRKPATRICK	(M)

1875 Wt. W593/826 1,000,000 4/15 J.B.C. & A. A.D.S.S./Forms/C. 2118.

WAR DIARY
or
INTELLIGENCE SUMMARY

Army Form C. 2118

Place	Date	Hour	Summary of Events and Information	Remarks and references to Appendices
@ CARNOY	Oct 26		was wounded in both legs, and Sgt MORLEY had his left foot completely blown away. The other injuries were slight. No 14593 Sgt MEEK received immediate medical treatment to Sgt MORLEY, and for the time saved his life. He unfortunately died 4 days later about ½pm as advance party was marching up to BRAY to take over billets, when they were shelled on the road – No 2 Lt FOY was wounded. He subsequently died in Hospital. Relieved by 12th Batt A & S Highlanders at 9pm – arrived in BRAY 10.30pm.	3
	Oct 27		Training and refitting at BRAY. Wet cold day. Marched out of BRAY at 4.30 pm, and billeted at VAUX sur SOMME. – Arrived in billets 7.30pm. These are the best billets we have been in. The people all so civil and anxious to help the men	1440
VAUX SUR SOMME	Oct 28		on a Battalion parade this morning I awarded the Regimental Military Medal of the prompt action of No 14593 Sgt MEEK. Wet day Training and refitting at VAUX.	1140
	29		do	1140

WAR DIARY
INTELLIGENCE SUMMARY

Army Form C. 2118

Place	Date	Hour	Summary of Events and Information	Remarks and references to Appendices
VILLERS BOCAGE	Oct 30th		Left VAUX at 9am to march to Brigade HQ at VILLERS BOCAGE. The new Brigadier (General HIBBERT) marched at the head of the Column. He inspected the Brigade as they marched through CORBIE. We halted at 11am for dinners just outside LA NOUVELLE and marched again at 2pm – The 79th Bde of our Divisn met us en route. On passing through QUERRIEUX the Turcos at BRAY. On passing through QUERRIEUX the 10th Army Corps Commander inspected us on the march. At ALLONVILLE the G.O.C. 26th Divn inspected us. Passed through FOISY and reached VILLERS BOCAGE at 5:30 p.m. (in the dark) Got into very indifferent billets. Only 1 man fell out on this 17 miles march – The Pipers, drums and Buglers did a lot to assist the men in marching. The Band was not been inspected before - & consist of 1 Piper major and 11 pipers. 1 Bass and 4 side drums & 22 Buglers. Report of new Brigadier 77th Inf. Bde attached at "A"	4
	31		Training and refitting at VILLERS BOCAGE	

NW Hampson Lt Col.

COPY.   11TH SCOTTISH RIFLES.

            Report of enemy's mining operations on morning
                        of 25-10-1915.

        About 1.45 a.m. an enemy's mine was exploded on the
right of 73 Trench: at the same time a sap head of ours was
destroyed on the left of 72 Trench.
        The explosion was accompanied by a heavy shell and
rifle fire.
        A new CRATER was formed in front of the right of 73
trench. This was occupied by the Brigade Grenadier Officer
and 2nd Lieut. Dangerfield of this Regiment, with about 10
regimental Bombers. They held the whole of the new CRATER,
until dawn; as it was found the enemy's old CRATER enfiladed
the new one - Major Davidson (who was in command) decided
to withdraw them.
        The enemy made no attempt to occupy the new CRATER.
        The damage done to our Trenches was as follows:-

        (a) 40 yards of No. 73 trench parapet driven in.

        (b) Practically the remaining parapet of 73 will
            have to be rebuilt, as the explosion drove
            the parapet back at least a foot.

        (c) 60 yards of No. 74 Trench requires repairing.

Casual-   One Officer, Scottish Rifles, was wounded in the wrist
ties.   whilst re-building parapet. No men were injured by explos-
        ion of mine: but the following casualties occurred in the
        Sap already mentioned.

                        Killed.

            1   R. E.
            3   Q. V. Rifles.
            ―
            4

                    Wounded.
            5   Scottish Rifles)   Gassed and
            3   Q. V. Rifles   )   injured.
            2   R. E.   )
           ――
           10

Artillery   The Observery Officer reported himself to me at 2.15
            a.m. I asked him to fire 8 rounds to protect my working
            party: 3 a.m.

Action   The O. C. in command of No. 2 Co. (73) Trench reported
taken.   to me at 2.10 a.m. of the explosion. I directed him to
            clear away the damaged parapet and at the same time sent him
            one platoon from my support with sand bags, picks and shovels
            to assist him.
                It was impossible to sap out to the new CRATER until the
            debris of the parapet and Listening posts had been cleared.

Reports.   Reports of mine explosion sent to Brigade H. Q. and to
            Royal Fusiliers and Scots Fusiliers.

Proposed   Repairing fire trenches in 73 and 74. Sapping out to
action.   new CRATER. Constructing and repairing old Listening Posts.

                        (Sd.) H. A. THOMPSON. Lieut. Col.
                    Commanding, 11th Scottish Rifles.
10 a. m.
25-10-15.

COPY.

GRENADIERS.

The Officer Commanding,
    11th Scottish Rifles.

With reference to your letter dated 25.10.15 bringing to the notice of the Brigadier-General Commanding the commendable work done by Lieut. Harding, Cheshire Regiment, 2nd Lieut. E. Dangerfield, Sergt. Geddes, Corporal Fisher and nine grenadiers of your Battalion during the night 24/25th October. With regard to Lieut. Harding a copy of your letter with remarks is being forwarded to 15th Brigade.

With regard to Lieut. Dangerfield hisname will be submitted for mention when the next list is called for. Please forward the names of the two most deserving rank and file from the 11 referred to, for submission along with the name of Lieut. Dangerfield.

The Brigadier-General Commanding wishes to express his appreciation of the highly commendable work done by your Grenadiers on that occasion.

(Sd.) W. CUNNINGHAM. Major.
Brigade Major, 77th Infantry Brigade.

31.10.15

Certified true copy
Roy Taylor Lt. of ADJUTANT,
11th (Serv.) Battn. The CAMERONIANS.
(SCOTTISH RIFLES)

COPY.

To

        Headquarters,

GRENADIERS.   77th Infantry Brigade.

In accordance with your 564 of 31-10-15.

I beg to submit the names of the following men as directed:-

No. 15463 CORPL DAVID FISHER.

No. 15417 PTE EDWARD PATTERSON.

I have published the remarks of the Brigadier-General in Battalion Orders, and wish to say how much my Regiment appreciates them.

                (Sd.) H. A. THOMPSON.

                          Lieut. Col.

        Commanding, 11th Scottish Rifles.

1-11-15.

Certified true Copy

W. T. Taylor Lt. & ADJUTANT,
11th (Serv.) Battn. The CAMERONIANS
(SCOTTISH RIFLES)

C O P Y.

The Officer Commanding,
    11th Scottish Rifles.

   The Brigadier-General Commanding directs me to say that he considers the action of No. 14,593 Sergt. Meek of your Battalion very commendable.

   His prompt action not only saved Sergt. Morley's life, but also set a fine example of coolness and sense of duty to the men.

                              (Sd.) W. CUNNINGHAM.   Major.
                         Brigade Major, 77th Infantry Brigade.

31-10-15.

Certified True Copy

Wm. S. Taylor. Lt. a/ ADJUTANT.
11th (Serv.) Battn. The CAMERONIANS.
            (SCOTTISH RIFLES)

C O P Y.

From

    Officer Commanding,

        11th The Cameronians (Scottish Rifles)

To

    Headquarters,

        77th Infantry Brigade.

    I forward herewith a report from the Medical Officer of my Regiment with reference to the prompt action of No. 14,593 Sergeant Meek, who saved the life of No. 14,430, Sergeant Morley, by immediately putting a tourniquet on the leg of the wounded man.

    Sergeant Meek had no previous medical training beyond the lectures delivered by Capt. Bourke, R. A. M. C., at Sutton Veny.

    I therefore wish to bring to the notice of the Brigadier General the prompt action of No. 14,593 Sergeant Meek.

                (Sd.) H. A. THOMPSON. Lieut.-Col.

                Commanding, 11th The Cameronians (Scottish Rifles).

28-10-15.

Certified true copy

Mr. Taylor, Lt. acting ADJUTANT.
11th (Serv.) Battn. The CAMERONIANS
(SCOTTISH RIFLES)

C O P Y.

29th October, 1915.

In accordance with your request, I have the honour to report, as follows, on the conduct of 14,593, Sergeant Meek, 11th Scottish Rifles:-

At about 1 p.m. on the 26th instant, No. 14,430 Sergeant Morley, 11th Scottish Rifles was hit by a German Rifle Grenade in the front line trench.

The whole of his left foot was blown away above the ankle joint.

Sergeant Meek immediately improvised a tourniquet from materials at hand and applied it to control the severe haemorrhage. This N.C.O. had no instruction beyond one lecture on first aid in England.

His promptitude and resource undoubtedly saved Sergeant Morley's life.

(Sd.) J. F. BOURKE, Capt. R.A.M.C.
Medical Officer.
11th The Cameronians (Scottish Rifles).

To

Officer Commanding,

11th The Cameronians (Scottish Rifles.

Certified true copy

Wm J Taylor Lt. act. ADJUTANT,
11th (Serv.) Battn. The CAMERONIANS.
(SCOTTISH RIFLES)

C O P Y.   77th Brigade.

The Brigadier-General Commanding wishes to express to all ranks in the Brigade his appreciation of the soldierly conduct and bearing of the Brigade during the recent attachment to the 5th Division, both when Battalions were under instruction with older Brigades and also latterly when the Brigade was holding Sector C.

11th S R
12th A & S
Highlrs
{ The two Battalions holding the left of the Sector had each the experience of a mine explosion.

On both occasions the behaviour of the Officers and other ranks was very creditable, and the prompt and energetic way in which the damage done was repaired showed the possession of that discipline which is essential to the reputation of a Regiment.

The Grenadiers of both Battalions showed their appreciation of what their duties are, by their immediate and fearless action.

10th D W
8th R S F
{ The two battalions holding the right of the Sector although they did not have the experience of mine explosions, carried out the duties which fell to their lot in an equally creditable manner.

The march of the Brigade yesterday was what a March should be. The Brigade having begun to make a reputation it behoves it to live up to it and add to it and not live on it.

(Sd.) W. CUNNINGHAM.   Major.
Brigade Major, 77th Infantry Brigade.

31-10-15.

Certified true Copy

Wm Taylor Lt act. ADJUTANT,
11th (Serv.) Battn. The CAMERONIANS.
(SCOTTISH RIFLES)

1.P

12/
7083

36th Division

12th Argylls
Vol I

Sept 15 + Oct

77/26

Issued III Army
[signature]
10/11/25

Army Form C. 2118.

WAR DIARY
or
INTELLIGENCE SUMMARY.
(Erase heading not required.)

Instructions regarding War Diaries and Intelligence Summaries are contained in F. S. Regs., Part II. and the Staff Manual respectively. Title pages will be prepared in manuscript.

Place	Date	Hour	Summary of Events and Information	Remarks and references to Appendices
Shorncliffe	Sept 17th	10 p.m	Transport & details left under Major Falconer Steward for Southampton & thence.	E.N.
Sutton Veny	" 19th	4.20 pm	Remainder of Battalion leave for Folkestone & Boulogne. Detained at Folkestone for 24 hours arrived	E.N.
Boulogne			Men embarked. Entrained at Boulogne after nights sleep for St Aubin. arrived	E.M.
	"21st"		Men marched 12½ miles to St Aubin, where billeted. Chiefs in barns.	
St Aubin	22.IX.15.		Resting. Men rather tired & go[ing] many bad feet.	E.N.
St Aubin	23.IX.15.	4-45 p.m.	Left St Aubin 3½ of an hour after to leave took 1 hr 30 min. March advisable but may men with bad feet. Broken down to one A.S.C. wagon which lifted. Arrived at Salarue at 1-20 am no billets	E.N.
Salarue	24.IX.15	8.30 a.m.	Men left at Brigade for Villers-Bretonneux. Route via Amiens: Inspected in march by Army Corps Commander. March Discipline bad, men taking off frequently. Billets had accommodation being very limited. All men in dry	E.N.
		4-30 p.m.		
Villers-Bretonneux	25.IX.15.	10-3.0 a.m.	Parade A[ny] & party Coy for ceremonial parade at Aerodrome. Remainder of men on billets.	E.N.
Villers-Bretonneux	26.IX.15.	12-4.5 p.m.	Battalion gassed by way of practice: all men in Gasmasks.	E.N.
"	27.IX.15	-	Battalion train meal.	E.N.
"	28.IX.15	-	Battalion drill. Received orders to man the attached to 27th Divn. Orders as suddenly cancelled at 9-15 pm.	E.N.
"	29.IX.15	-	Battn training.	E.N.
"	30.IX.15	-	Battn training. Route marched to Warfusée-Abancourt in afternoon when the 1st Battn were in Rest Camp. Spent an	E.N.
Villers-Bret[onneux]	1.X.15		hour with them	E.N.
	2.X.15	9.10 a.m.	Battn left for Cappy. Bivouaced for dinner at Herrecourt. Arrived in Cappy attached to 80th Bde at 8 p.m. Billets.	E.N.
Cappy	3.X.15	6-15 p.m.	Officers over trenches in morning. Battn marched as a Platoons at 6-15 p.m. R[igh]t½ B[atta]lt[n] attached to 3rd K.R.R.C.	E.N.
	4.X.15	-	Men guard :- 15 casualties in evening, one of whom was sent to hospital. The remainder rejoined Batt[n]. Billeted for	E.N.
"	5.X.15	-	the night 5th/6th in Cappy.	E.N.
"	6.X.15	4-30 am	Left Cappy for Villers-BRETTONEAUX. Bivouaced at Méricourt for breakfast. Arrival in billets at 1 pm.	E.N.

26th Division

12th Inf: Rect Dept 72
Vol 2

Oct 15.

Army Form C. 2118.

WAR DIARY
or
INTELLIGENCE SUMMARY.
(Erase heading not required.)

Instructions regarding War Diaries and Intelligence Summaries are contained in F.S. Regs., Part II. and the Staff Manual respectively. Title pages will be prepared in manuscript.

Place	Date	Hour	Summary of Events and Information	Remarks and references to Appendices
VILLERS-BRETTONEUX	7.X.15.		Batt. training. Inspected by III (Corps Commander).	E.M.
"	8.X.15		Batt. training.	E.M.
"	9.X.15		Batt. training. Church parade.	E.M.
"	10.X.15		Batt. training.	E.M.
"	11.X.15		Batt. inspection. Church parade.	E.M.
"	12.X.15	4-20 p.m.	Left VILLERS-BRETTONEUX for SAILLY-LORETTE. Went into billets there. 14 men left with Advance Gr. det.	E.M.
SAILLY-LORETTE	13.X.15	4-20 p.m.	Left for BRAY. Arrived BRAY at 4.25 p.m.	E.M.
BRAY	14.X.15	5-15 p.m.	Relieved 4th CHESHIRES in Subsector G. Relief carried out well. At 8.20 just on completion enemy exploded a mine, after rapid fire, followed by some shelling. Men stood to well, worked at repair all night. Enemy quiet. Casualties 1 killed, 4 wounded.	E.M.
Trenches G2.	15.X.15		Working on repair of trench aids. Enemy repeated.	BM
"	16.X.15		Enemy Quiet. No report of a rumour of attack on front of III Army.	BM
"	17.X.15	5-15 p.m.	Somewhat noisy night. But night was particularly quiet. Trench mortars form 4th CHESHIRES Relieved by 1st CHESHIRES. Relief took 1hr + 25 minutes.	BM
BRAY.	18.X.15	5-35.	Batt. arrived & took down Batt. attain position in battle position. Casualties. This relieved 1 better than the average of the regiment.	E.M.
"	19.X.15	7-25 p.m.	to Bivouac.	E.M.
Trenches G2	20.X.15	7 p.m.	Relieved 1st CHESHIRES. Relief went through smoothly and enemy kept quiet all night.	E.M.
"	21.X.15		Very quiet day. Lot of work done on RESERVE trench. Enemy seen working from Aveler. A lot of grenades in aware as relandstone for attack to bombers on a rifle battery located in the morning. Casualties 1 Killed & 1 wounded.	E.M.
"	22.X.15		Quiet all day.	
BRAY	23.X.15	10 p.m.	Quiet day. 1st Scottish Rifles relieved us. Relief quite smooth. A mine was reported opposite 74 F.T. on lamp but did not go off. Some butch in RP.44.	E.M.

Army Form C. 2118.

WAR DIARY
or
INTELLIGENCE SUMMARY.
(Erase heading not required.)

Instructions regarding War Diaries and Intelligence Summaries are contained in F. S. Regs., Part II. and the Staff Manual respectively. Title pages will be prepared in manuscript.

Place	Date	Hour	Summary of Events and Information	Remarks and references to Appendices
BRAY.	24.x.15.	—	Heavy fatigues all day on 2nd line works.	E.A.
"	25.x.15.	—	Fatigues.	E.A.
Trenches C2	26.x.15.	7 p.m.	Relieved 11th Scottish Rifles in same sector. Relief was reported well completed. Enemy artillery active. A mine had been blown up opposite 73 STREET. Work done by trenches in consolidating F.T. with crater & sap; other work clearing front wire.	E.A.
"	27.x.15.	—	Enemy quiet. Mine opposite 74 F.T. still reported ready to go off. Casualties 1 killed, 1 wounded.	E.A.
BRAY.	28.x.15.	7 p.m.	Relieved by 1st NORFOLKS. It had been raining all day & trenches were undesirable. Went into same billets	E.A.
"			in BRAY.	
S. AILLY-LORETTE	29.x.15.	4.30 p.m.	Packed up in morning & moved to SAILLY-LORETTE. Marched past Sir N.M. Stewart for last time	E.A.
CORSY.	30.x.15.	2.30 p.m.	Left SAILLY-LORETTE for 28th Div. Area. Formed up on Rode at VAUX-SUR-SOMME & Gen. under new General. — : Route CORBIE – LANGUEVILLE – QUERRIEUX – AILLONVILLE – Chalfinche. We were inspected en route by Divisional Brigadier at CORBIE. By 16th Corps Commander at QUERRIEUX & the 28th Divel General after leaving AILLONVILLE. Billets rather poor.	F.Y.
"	31.x.15.		Wet. Day spent in improving billets.	E.N.

www.ingramcontent.com/pod-product-compliance
Lightning Source LLC
Chambersburg PA
CBHW081541160426
43191CB00011B/1810